Trucking Company

2021-22

The Ultimate Guide to Easily Start & Grow a Profitable Owner-Operator Business Nowadays. Use the Latest Strategies to Run and Automate Operations & Build a Thriving Fleet

Zachary Bosch

Zachary Bosch

Table of Contents

Zachary Bosch

Introduction

Have you been working for a trucking company for a while and have been dabbling with the idea of becoming an owner-operator? Making the switch from an employee for a carrier to running your own business is tough. There are many administrative hurdles you'll have to cross, and it can seem intimidating if you don't know where to begin. Even if you do manage to set yourself up legally, there's the small matter of finding clients who will hire you. Being an independent business owner is one of the most fulfilling things you can do in life. It gives you the freedom to set your hours and to firmly control your financial destiny. Freedom is what we're all after at the end of the day, and in this book, my aim is to show you how you can set yourself free. Becoming an owner-operator might seem hard, but I assure you that it all comes down to following the right processes. If you've heard horror stories in the past of people who failed to establish their own business, don't worry. Misfortune struck them probably because they didn't take the time to educate themselves. This is a disconcertingly common experience that happens to many truckers who make the leap to becoming owner-operators. Having worked in the industry for a while, they think they know everything about the business and that they can easily make money. The reality is that to make money and be successful, you need to first educate yourself. It's a bit like trying to become a doctor without going to medical school. In this case, you'll end up harming yourself and will have to return to working a job to bring some money in.

It's true that there are many steps involved in successfully running your owner-operator business. However, this book is going to walk you through all of them while giving you practical information that you can use at all times. This isn't a book that's going to throw jargon at you. In some cases, I might use words that you'll need to familiarize yourself with because that's the nature of the business. However, this book is written in easy-to-follow English that will leave you without any doubts as to how you can go about running a successful business.

One of the most powerful ways of running your business is to have your operations run on autopilot. You won't have time to make money if all you're doing is chasing paperwork and responding to mundane questions all the time. I'm going to show you how you can automate the mundane stuff and focus on what really makes you money in this business.

What You'll Learn

In addition to automating certain business tasks, you're going to learn about the basics of the trucking industry. It seems funny to say this, but most truckers have no idea how their industry came to be. While a full-fledged history lesson isn't going to help you, it pays for you to understand how the industry has evolved and will continue to evolve in the future. This will help you best position yourself in terms of competitive advantage.

The trucking business aims to solve certain problems, and in the first chapter, I'm going to walk you through all of them. You'll also learn what you can expect on the job and how much you can expect to earn. Most truckers have no idea about what sort of income they could be making, and choosing to start a business without getting a handle on the kind of money you can make is a surefire way to doom yourself.

Next, you'll learn all about the administrative side of your business. This is going to seem boring, but it's necessary. You need to incorporate it as a legal structure to safeguard both yourself and your customers. A legal structure also gives you credibility, and it's essential that you establish this when starting out.

Licensing and permits are perennial issues in the world of trucking, and I'll walk you through everything you need to do to succeed. You've probably heard of FMCSA if you've been in the business for a while. It's now time to get to know them better since they're the body that will regulate your activities. Understanding how they work and how you can stay on their good side is essential to running a successful business. I'm going to show you that all the paperwork is actually quite simple to deal with. Equipment and insurance are the next topics you'll learn about in this book. The wrong equipment can break your business. More importantly, you need to figure out what's right for you and the kinds of loads you're looking to carry. It's no good showing up in a van to haul HAZMAT loads. This sort of thing happens more often than you might realize and is why shippers immediately turn to freight brokers. Building trust is essential, and your equipment along with the right insurance policy to back your operation up are also essential.

Ask most truckers what they think the business consists of, and they'll say "driving". Yes, driving's a part of it, but there are a ton of mundane tasks that you need to get done. I'll show you how you can organize these tasks and make life easy for yourself. I'll also give you all of the costs associated with this business so you won't have any surprises going in.

Lastly, you'll need to automate a lot of tasks to squeeze the most out of your time. The more time you spend attracting customers and marketing yourself, the more money you'll make. You can even put yourself in a position to start a fleet. A business plan is essential for scaling your business, and I'm going to walk you through a sample plan that will help you raise money and build credibility.

As great as all of these things are, they're information at the end of the day, and it's only as good as what you make of it. It's intimidating to set out on your own, but trust me when I say that the rewards are immense. There will be tough times, but maintaining focus steadfastly on your goals will get you through them. If you're willing to do what's needed to become successful, you're going to find this business to be one of the most rewarding endeavors of your life. So, are you ready to expand your career and become a bonafide business owner? Are you ready to create a life of freedom for yourself? If your answer is yes, let's move on to the first chapter and take a look at the origins of the trucking industry.

Chapter 1:
The Trucking Industry

You see trucks everywhere on the roads. They're one of the oldest and most reliable forms of transportation in America. The people who operate trucks work different hours from normal workers. Individuals have always needed goods delivered to them, and the modes of transport have changed over the years. Steam-powered boats were the first mass freight moving machines but were limited for obvious reasons.

Transportation by land was carried out on horseback, but by the arrival of the 1900s, trucks began replacing horse carriages. Back then, it took a truck one month to travel from Seattle to New York. They were cumbersome and weren't much faster than an ant. However, technological developments meant that by the late 1920s, the horse carriage was pretty much extinct. In the early days of trucking, states viewed them with distrust. They were thought to damage roads due to their massive weight, and some states limited them to 28,000 pounds. The two world wars changed people's impression of trucks. Pneumatic tires (which contain air) were trialed, and the trucking industry was truly on its way. After World War II, America had over a million trucks on its roads. Roads improved, and the diesel engine was introduced. In 1956, the federal government committed to building the interstate highway system which allowed for the development of bigger trucks that could travel at higher speeds. A long trailer design was adopted because this was deemed the safest option. Somewhere along the way, the modern behemoths you see on the roads came into existence. Trucking has been the lifeblood of America's logistics industry. Rail freight is limited to certain industrial goods. Trucking picks up the slack for the rest of the country. It's responsible for turning a cluster of local state economies into a giant and efficient economic machine. These days, 70% of all freight transported in the United States happens via trucks. This translates to around $700 billion on goods shipped annually. If you're looking to get into the trucking industry, here's some good news: there's almost always a driver shortage. The reasons for this aren't tough to figure out. Trucking requires you to put in unconventional hours and keeps you on the road for the majority of your time. Most people are accustomed to working for a few hours per day and coming home to their families in the evening.

A trucker sets more unconventional hours and has to manage their time better. Indeed, as you'll learn later in this book, successful trucking is all about time management.

How Does It Work?

So how does the trucking business work? On the surface, it's quite simple. People need freight moved, so they call a trucker and have goods delivered from one destination to another. However, it's not as simple as that. There are a ton of safety and legal procedures that need to be followed before anything gets delivered. You might also be wondering why these companies don't simply call delivery services such as FedEx and UPS. Well, some of them do.

However, once a manufacturer starts producing goods on a massive scale, it makes more sense for them to coordinate their own logistics. This gives them more control over their operations and allows them to dictate delivery times precisely to their customers. Setting up an entire logistics wing is a tough task. Large companies produce and move more freight than the biggest trucking fleet in America. However, the number of such companies is low.

It's far more common to find companies that produce just enough goods to justify starting a logistics operation of their own, but not enough to justify them building their own fleet. This is where truckers come into the picture. Usually, the logistics arm of these companies networks with freight brokers to find reliable carriers. If a trucking company has established relationships with them, the customer works with the trucker directly.

Bigger customers are loath to work with truckers directly because they have varying needs. For example, they might have a single shipment that needs to be broken into multiple batches and delivered to different locations at different times. A single trucking company is going to find it difficult to do all this. As a result, freight brokers have an entry into the system, and they're the ones you'll be dealing with for the most part as a trucker. Let's look at how they and other cogs in the logistics machine work.

Freight Brokers

Freight brokers are industry mainstays that coordinate shipments between customers and truckers. Some truckers resent them since they're a middleman that takes a commission on the services that truckers provide. However, this is a short-sighted view to take. A good freight broker acts effectively as your marketing division, and you won't have to ever worry about scoring a load or having to find an easy load to make your way back home. Some truckers think freight brokers don't do anything since the trucker is the one who does all the physical driving while the broker usually operates through a phone. This is a bit like saying that anyone who works in an office doesn't do real work. You should view freight brokers as your partners in the business. Having said that, there are unscrupulous brokers out there who will try to squeeze you on rates as much as possible. No one's forcing you to work with such businesses. A key aspect of successful trucking is finding the right counterparties to deal with. Many truckers sign up to drive for less than reliable parties and find themselves without anything to show for it. They then complain that everyone in the business is bad. The problem is that they made a poor choice right at the start. I can't guarantee you'll never have a bad experience. However, if you follow the steps found in this book, you'll end up attracting the right kinds of customers to you most of the time. Either way, freight brokers add a lot of value to the system. Customers love them because brokers tend to have a high-level view of the industry. They are usually aware of trucking conditions and prices across multiple states as well as the laws that govern shipments in them. A single trucker will find it hard to provide this degree of information to a client. Good freight brokers also nurture their carriers. After all, the broker is judged by the work that the carrier does. Freight brokers are always on the lookout for reliable carriers, and they're a great way to find steady work when you begin. You'll have to give up a portion of your fee to work with them, but they make up for it in volumes.

Manufacturers and Shippers

These entities are the ones who need freight shipped. The kinds of goods they need to ship are varied, and they exist all across the country. You might find more natural resources and HAZMAT oriented shippers in the southwest, while the shippers of the midwest might be more agricultural in nature. Whatever the load, the shipper is the customer at the end of the day and pays everyone else in the logistics chain. Large manufacturers will have their own logistics division as I mentioned previously. However, the majority of shippers won't have their fleet. Smaller manufacturers will even work with individual truckers or small fleet operating companies. The logistics business changes depending on where the shipper is located. As a trucker, you can't always control who you end up working with because of this. Your home base might have a large number of manufacturers who work with truckers directly, but on backhauls (return trips) you might have to accept business from a freight broker. So, always keep your options open. You can guarantee a better rate for yourself by picking the right niche. I'll talk about this later in the book.

Freight Forwarders

These companies are typically large operators and manage their own fleets. Every now and then, they might require an independent operator to haul loads to an area they don't service.

However, they usually aren't a steady source of loads for the average trucker. A freight forwarding company gathers customer freight at a sorting facility and then breaks it up into smaller shipments to different locations.

They can also consolidate smaller shipments into one large shipment to a single location. At the core of the freight forwarding business is the warehouse. While transportation is an important part of it, the warehouse is where the sorting and organization happens. From a truck owner-operator's point of view, it doesn't hurt to approach freight forwarders to check if they have loads for you. Just don't expect to make a steady living off of them.

What to Know Before Getting Started

Before we dive into what you need to do to get started in the trucking business, it's important for you to understand a few things. Many people get into trucking only to find out that it's much tougher than they ever expected and isn't suited for them. Below, we will go over the most important things you need to know before you make the switch to an owner-operator.

It's Tough

This book is going to help you make the jump to an owner-operator, but it's not as if this is an easy business to crack. The toughness emerges not from the things you need to do but from the fact that you'll have to put in long hours. The economics of the business also aren't in your favor, and you'll need to rack up a lot of miles to make money. This sort of arrangement isn't always suitable for most people.

Most truckers live unconventional lives that normal people struggle to understand. You won't have a day job where you can sit at a desk and chat with your coworkers. If you've already worked as a driver you'll know that you won't have coworkers other than the ones you randomly bump into on the road; you won't have normal hours like a nine to five where you can clock out and then go home to your family. Now, imagine adding the stress of finding your own loads and figuring out your schedule for yourself. It can get stressful if you don't do the right things. It shouldn't come as a surprise that most truckers neglect planning and simply wing their loads. This is why you hear stories of burnt-out truckers who never wish to see their cabs ever again. You need to love planning in advance to have any sort of success as a trucker.

If you're someone who wants everything to be figured out for you in advance, then it's going to be tough for you to succeed. Successful truckers are mentally strong people who are willing to do what it takes to succeed in their business.

It's More Than Just Money

Money is important, and you can make quite a lot of it with careful planning. However, if you focus too much on the money, you'll end up creating an imbalance in your life. You need to place importance on your personal and family life along with your need to make money. True success lies in managing and balancing both needs. There are truckers out there who make a ton of money, but they aren't what you'd call successful. Sleeping in your cab 300 days a year isn't anyone's idea of success no matter how much money is made.

This is where planning comes into the picture. You need to be realistic about how much money you can make given the sort of family life you want. I'm not saying you should not prioritize making money—far from it. However, always keep the need for a balance in mind. You'll be able to prioritize your loads better and more effectively maximize your earnings and time.

The Margins Are Thin

This is something that no one else will tell you before you enter the business. You'll be sold an independent lifestyle on the road and shown scenic pictures of mountains with solitary trucks on them. All of that is true; however, the good cannot exist without the bad. The margins in the trucking industry are thin as they are everywhere in the logistics business. This is why moving huge volumes makes more money.

When trucking, it's best to adopt Murphy's law as your anthem. Murphy's law asserts that everything that can go wrong usually will. You'll have a tire blowout that will delay your delivery leading to a penalty, for example, or some misguided driver in a car will decide to change lanes right as you're accelerating and cause you to stress your brake lines. Or perhaps your truck will develop some issue in the middle of nowhere requiring a fix that will stress your margins, or DOT officials will find something wrong on your truck that puts you out of compliance and you'll have to spend more money to fix it. The list of possibilities goes on and on. The biggest issue you'll have is that you'll struggle to collect your full invoice amount. This is because of the prevalence of credit cycles in the logistics business. Customers typically pay on a cycle of 30 to 60 days or even longer which means you'll have to use a factoring company. These companies pay you 90% of your invoice amount up front and the remaining 10% when the customer pays. They'll charge you between one and three percent of your invoice. When you consider that your net margin is 10% to begin with, a 3% hit on your collection is significant. Cash is king in a trucking business, so you shouldn't jump into it unless you have enough reserves to tide you over in case things go awry. I'll detail all of the costs later in this book, but for now, prepare to have at least 60-90 days worth of running expenses as cash in your account.

Systems and Processes

Technically, this point applies to pretty much every business out there, but it's especially relevant for trucking. Without a system in place, you're not going to be able to run your business the way it ought to be run. You'll find yourself forever scrambling to put things in place, and you won't have any cash to pay for your unexpected expenses. Then there's the fact that as an owner-operator, you'll have to file administrative records and handle your taxes. Your best friends in this business will be an accountant, an insurance agent, and a lawyer, in some cases. Without these three professionals in your corner, you're going to find it very hard to run your business profitably. Not only do they make things easier for you, they'll also protect you when things go wrong. Many truckers underestimate the value that these professionals bring to their business and think they can handle everything themselves. This is the worst way to be in this business. You'll have a lot on your plate, and expecting yourself to be able to handle things you have no idea about is a surefire way to fail.

So, do you still want to be a trucker? Don't let these negatives scare you away. There are many positives about the business that you should be equally aware of. Here they are in no particular order.

Pay

One of the biggest pros of the trucking business is the pay. You'll find that the average salary is mentioned online as $35,000 for a new trucker. However, this figure takes low demand areas into account. In areas that witness high traffic, your starting salary will be north of $50,000. Experienced truckers can earn as much as $100,000 per year. The figures for owner-operators are more difficult to estimate since so much depends on how they run their business. However, it's reasonable to expect to earn six figures per year. How high those six figures go depends on the way you structure your business and the kind of loads you carry. If you happen to transport HAZMAT loads, the pay is extremely high, but you'll have to contend with more compliance, for example.

As an owner-operator, you won't have access to the immense benefits that trucking companies provide, but you can sign up for better health insurance plans thanks to the money you make. Often, you can negotiate bonuses with long-term clients, and this will add to your earnings.

The Open Road

Being OTR, or on the open road, is the primary pull for most truckers. Your office will be mother nature, and as far as scenery goes, it's pretty hard to beat that. While most people will be stuck behind their desks, forced into cubicles, you'll have all the fresh air you want.

I'm not saying driving a truck is a pleasant experience at all times, but the feeling of freedom that the open road gives you is unmatched, and trucking is one of the only professions that gives you this feeling.

If you're someone who loves exploring new areas and traveling, then trucking is a great way to fulfill this desire.

Independence

As a truck owner-operator, no one dictates terms to you. You're your own boss, and the buck stops with you. This might be scary for some since they can't handle the feeling of responsibility, but if you're thinking of becoming an owner, chances are you have what it takes. After all, such impulses don't come to random people. You won't have to deal with middle managers micromanaging your work in a bid to impress their bosses.

You set your schedule, choose which loads you want to transport, and schedule your own routes. If there's a particularly scenic route you want to take on the way to your destination, then feel free to take this. Your customer will have a GPS feed of your progress, but as long as you're on time, no one's going to bother you to hurry up. What's more, the government is on your side when it comes to setting your hours. Safety is an extremely important issue, and as you'll shortly learn, the hours you spend driving are central to it.

Community

Truckers are one giant brotherhood. There is a certain sense of camaraderie you'll develop with your fellow truckers since you're all in it together. Other truckers will also be some of your best sources of loads and tips when on the road. Truck stops are full of people exchanging tips and engaging in shop talk. Often, you'll run into people you haven't seen in a while in some far-flung place on the map. Many people think trucking is a lonely and solitary industry. However, this isn't the case. Sure, you will spend long hours in your cab, but there's no reason for you to remain there forever. Step out of your cab, and there's always someone waiting to welcome you, wherever you are!

Security

Normal office workers are perennially worried about job security. Their companies can instantly replace them with someone else. However, the trucking industry is facing a shortage of qualified drivers. This is great news for you as an owner-operator. It means demand is greater than supply, and you'll likely have no problems finding work as long as you adhere to the proper safety standards. Which other industry or job can boast such conditions? Not many. As a truck owner, you'll be fully in charge, and as long as you handle your affairs correctly, as I'll show you in this book, an extremely successful business awaits you.

Women and Trucking

Trucking is one of those industries that happen to be male-dominated. Starting a business is hard enough, but it can be especially intimidating for a woman to manage her business and enter a male-dominated field. The processes that you need to execute to make your business a success are the same as what a man needs to do. Moreover, there is a growing number of women who are entering trucking due to the driver shortage. There has never been a better time for a woman to enter trucking than right now. A particular challenge that women face is a good work-life balance. It can be hard to start a family when you're on the road for weeks at a time. Women also need to make sure they have access to safe parking zones and work in a safe environment. In the past, there were instances of women being harassed by their male trainers, but thankfully, the situation is getting much better these days. The industry isn't where it needs to be, but progress is being made. To this end, there are a few organizations that support women in trucking. The largest organization was founded in 2007 and is called Women in Trucking, or WIT. WIT is a non-profit that supports the hiring of women in trucking and seeks to minimize the obstacles a woman faces. The organization hosts networking events and other invitation-only events where truckers can connect with other women in the industry. REAL Women in Trucking is another organization that has done great work in promoting the inclusion of women in trucking. Founded in 2010, the group was originally formed to protest against unsafe work conditions women faced in the industry. They host a support network that promotes transparency in the workplace for women and mentors qualified women as they grow their careers. Finally, the Women and Girls in Transportation Initiative seeks to increase the participation of women in the trucking industry. It aims to prepare young women for a career in the industry by creating opportunities for them through internships, career placements, and so on. All of these associations have websites so reach out to them and join their network. No business is without challenges, but you should certainly not allow the fact that you're a woman to discourage you from becoming a trucker. You will have to lean on your support network more than the average man does, but there are many resources available to support you. There is greater awareness in the industry these days, and you'll find that the hurdles faced as a woman are fewer than what they were even five years ago. This wraps up our look at the trucking industry and the various players in it. As you can see, there is more to it than it seems on the surface. While it's a challenging career, there are many advantages as well. You need to understand both the pros and cons before embarking on starting your business. If you've worked as a driver before, you probably know all of this already. However, understand that your challenges will only increase because you'll have to deal with the existing issues plus those that plague a business owner. Make sure all of the advantages make it worthwhile for you. There's no doubt that trucking is a rewarding industry. However, these rewards need to match your mindset and outlook on what constitutes success and reward.

Zachary Bosch

Chapter 2:
Business Entities
and Administrative Issues

Most beginners to the trucking business think that all there is to it is leasing a truck and starting to drive. Unfortunately, there's a lot more included in the process. The truck or equipment is a big part of your business, but it isn't the only thing that's important. You need to make sure that your company has a good foundation from which you can build. This means you need to incorporate yourself using the right legal structure. There are many legal structures you can choose for your business, and all of them have their own advantages and disadvantages. On the surface, this material might seem like it's irrelevant; however, it's a critical part of being a business owner. To succeed as an owner-operator, you need to stop thinking as just a driver and begin thinking like a business owner.

You control your destiny when you run your own business, but this also means you have to bear greater responsibility.

So, take the time to understand all of the legal options you have for your business. You need to learn this stuff just once, so don't worry about having to deal with this forever. Let's begin by looking at the most basic form in which you can incorporate your business: sole proprietorship.

Sole Proprietorship

Sole proprietors are the most commonly found business owners in America, and there's a good reason for this. A sole proprietorship, or sole prop, is the easiest way for you to begin conducting business.

You don't have to file any notifications with the government. All you do is go about your business, and the moment from which you start earning money, you're officially in business.

While a sole prop might be easy to form and run, this doesn't mean it's automatically a good choice for everyone. Sole props are sometimes referred to as unincorporated businesses.

These businesses are run by a single person, and there is no formal document that indicates you're running a business, such as a state-issued license of any kind. Keep in mind that you'll still need permits to run a trucking business if you're a sole prop; it's just that you don't have to file any notification of conducting business with the IRS. A sole prop lacks liability protection.

This means there's no division between your business assets and personal ones. If someone sues you in court for damages, your personal assets such as property and money held in your personal accounts that aren't connected to your business, are also in play. This makes sole props a risky proposition for most truckers.

Sole Prop Taxation

Taxation is fairly straightforward with a sole prop. Since there is no division between your personal and business assets, all income that you earn from your business is considered personal income, and you'll pay taxes according to the marginal tax rate bracket that you fall under (Warnes, 2020). Filing taxes as a sole prop is pretty simple. You'll need to file IRS Form 1040 Schedule C. You're allowed to claim deductions to your income related to the expenses you incur running your business. Something to note here is that sole props pay self-employment taxes such as social security and Medicare, and this amounts to 15.3% of one's income. Sole props are not a good fit for truckers due to the immense risk of being hit with a liability claim. If anything goes wrong with your shipment or if you end up being part of an accident on the road, you'll be opening your personal assets to seizure. As a result, I'm not going to focus too much on sole props in this book. Instead, let's move on and take a look at another business structure you can choose.

Limited Liability Company (LLC)

LLCs are an easy business structure to incorporate under and provide you with immense benefits. For starters, they give you something that a sole prop doesn't, which is liability protection. Traditionally, liability protection was something only corporations enjoyed. However, corporations are expensive to run and maintain. The LLC combines the benefits of a sole prop with those of a corporation. It is a separate business entity from the individual who owns it. This means that your LLC's assets are separate from your personal ones.

The LLC is a pass-through entity. This means that all of the money it earns is passed through to its owners. The profits and losses that you earn will be included in your personal income tax return. This is a major benefit of the LLC since it helps you avoid double taxation. An LLC owner can also elect to be taxed as a corporation. This makes it an extremely flexible business entity. It should come as no surprise that the LLC is the preferred vehicle of choice for most owner-operators. Once you begin managing a fleet of trucks, a corporation might make more sense. However, in most cases, the LLC is a perfect vehicle. Running an LLC is much easier than running a corporation. This is due to the fact that corporations require a Board of Directors and a fully functioning accounting unit. LLCs don't need either, although they will require the help of an accountant.

Formation

An LLC has to be formally incorporated with the Secretary of State. You can incorporate an LLC anywhere in the continental United States. There's no law that says you have to file one in the state in which you reside. Delaware and Wyoming are the most common jurisdictions in which they're formed. The first step to forming an LLC is to check the availability of your business name. Some states will require you to add a suffix such as "company" or "limited" to your business' name. Next, you'll have to hire a registered agent. This agent is the entity responsible for receiving notice of a lawsuit and other legal actions against your business. The agent will have to be registered in the state in which your LLC is formed.

In the logistics business, registered agents are also referred to as process agents. They'll need to file the Form BOC-3 before you can begin conducting business. I'll explain everything to do with forms and processes in the next chapter. For now, just understand that a registered/process agent is a necessity for you to do business.

The next step is to file your articles of organization. This document is also referred to as the articles of formation or the certificate of formation. You'll need to file this with the Secretary of State. Once the articles are approved, you're officially ready to conduct business in the state.

This document is an extremely important one as it lays out how your LLC will be governed.

Here is the information it must include at a minimum:

- Name: Your LLC's name must be clearly spelled out
- Registered agent and their office address
- Management structure: LLCs can be member-managed or manager-managed. The former designation means the owners of the LLC (members) will be equally responsible for the running of the company. A manager-managed LLC has one person who's responsible for the operations.
- Membership certificates: Indicate whether your LLC uses membership certificates or not
- Effective date: The date on which the LLC becomes effective. The default date is when the Secretary processes your articles. You can indicate another date if you so choose.
- Duration: The default duration is in perpetuity. However, you can specify a dissolution date if you desire.
- Formed under: Each state has a corporation code that you need to designate. If you're using the state's template, a code will be mentioned automatically. This section isn't very relevant to you and mostly applies to certain types of LLCs such as professional LLCs, non-profit LLCs, and series LLCs.
- Organizers: The organizer is the individual who is responsible for executing the articles of organization. This person must sign the articles as well. You can have one or multiple organizers.
- Principal office: This is the business address of your company. It can be the same as your registered agent's address.
- Execution: All organizers must sign the execution statement of the articles. Typically, this is a code of honor that states that all information provided is correct under penalties of perjury.

All of this sounds complicated. The good news is most business owners don't have to concern themselves with the articles of incorporation. You can hire a lawyer to do it for you, or you can have your registered agent take care of the entire process for you. In fact, when creating an LLC, you can use a service that will file all necessary paperwork with the state and act as your registered agent. You'll pay a few hundred dollars more for these services, but it's worth the price.

If you've decided to go into business with partners, then you'll have to formally decide how all of you will split the relevant duties and create an operating agreement. You'll also have to hold an official first meeting of the members and file the notes of this meeting with the secretary. This meeting is when you'll decide to open a bank account and begin conducting operations. If you designate one person as the manager of the LLC, then this decision will have to be formally recorded as well.

If you're going to do business by yourself, then you don't have to do anything beyond filing the operating agreement with the state. Once this is done, you'll have to fill out Form SS-4 and apply for an Employer Identification Number, or EIN. This will function as your tax ID, and you'll have to mention this number in every tax filing you make with the IRS. Generally, the IRS takes up to 60 days to formally activate your EIN. You'll receive your EIN in the mail. However, the IRS automatically assigns you a number when you file the form. To get this number, you can call the IRS. Once you verify you're the owner of the company, they'll give you the EIN. You won't be able to use it immediately, but it can help you open a bank account on a provisional basis until the IRS fully activates it. Depending on the state in which you incorporate, you might run into a few additional requirements.

For example, some states require you to file an initial report with the Secretary. Some states require an annual or even semi-annual report. In some states, you'll have to file a notice of formation in a newspaper, as quaint as that sounds these days. The county office will give you the details of the publications. California imposes a franchise tax of $800 for conducting business in the state. This is a minimum tax. Similarly, Delaware has a tax of $300 per year.

Taxation

As I mentioned earlier, LLCs are pass-through entities. This means their income is considered the same as their personal income, and they won't have to file taxes for the company separately.

All profits, losses, deductions, and credits pass through to your personal income, and you'll have to include all of them on your personal income tax return at the end of the year. Your LLC will also have to pay state income taxes and other business-related taxes such as self-employment taxes. It's best to hire an accountant to file them.

Advantages of an LLC

An LLC is an easy company to incorporate. States charge different fees and it varies from $50 to $500. On average, you can expect to spend $200 if you choose to do it yourself. There are a few other fees you'll have to pay depending on the state. However, the process is extremely simple and there are many services that support you in this. The second advantage of an LLC is that it offers you pass-through taxation. Unlike a corporation that pays taxes twice, you won't be doubly charged. This means you get to keep more of your money while enjoying the benefits of running a business. Even if you have multiple members in the LLC, it's easy to define the proportion in which profits will be divided.

The operating agreement outlines all of this and it's easy to hire an attorney to craft this agreement for you. If the pass-through taxation model doesn't suit you, you can always elect to be taxed as a corporation. As your business grows, it might make more sense to elect corporation-like tax treatment. Thus, the LLC has an inbuilt mechanism that supports your growth. This in contrast to the sole prop structure where you'll run into issues when you begin to grow.

Unlike sole props, LLCs give you liability protection. If there's one advantage worth signing up for as a trucker, it's this. Liability protection means your personal assets will be insulated from lawsuits. Just make sure you separate your personal and business accounts. Some people choose to combine them, and this might result in you losing liability protection. Despite all of these advantages, there are a few disadvantages that you must be aware of.

Disadvantages of an LLC

LLCs are a relatively new form of company, with the first LLC being formed in the 1970s. This means the operating agreement assumes inordinate importance when it comes to governance issues since there isn't enough case law to set a precedent. This isn't a problem by itself but if you don't take care to define the terms of the agreement properly, you will run into major issues down the road.

The other issue with the LLC is that if you're aiming to raise cash from outside investors, then you'll find it difficult to do so. This happens because an LLC cannot issue shares of itself like a corporation can. An investor will have to become a member. While this isn't an issue by itself, the problem occurs when the investor wishes to exit their investment. During this time, it's most likely that the LLC will have to dissolve which leaves the other members in a poor position. In some cases, it might be possible to buy out the investor that wishes to leave but it's a tough process and there isn't a straightforward way to do it. As a result, most investors choose to simply not invest in an LLC and pick a corporation instead.

As your business grows, you might find that the LLC business structure constrains you. The inability to issue shares will hamper growth as will the way in which taxes are treated. By having everything pass through to the members, there's no room left for the company to save money and reinvest in itself tax-free. This is an advantage that corporations enjoy but LLCs pay taxes on every single dollar they earn. Even if you choose to elect to be taxed as a corporation, the benefits only go so far.

Thus, once your business grows it might be better to form a corporation. Despite all of these disadvantages though, there's no doubt an LLC is the best structure for a truck owner-operator when they're starting out.

Corporations

Corporations are a step up in terms of business structures. While LLCs are great, they do have their limitations when your business grows large. Corporations are legal entities that are fully separate from their owners. While LLCs are also separate, they incorporate the pass-through taxation method. Corporations don't do this. As far as the law is concerned, they're legal persons that are fully liable for their actions. This means you receive complete liability protection. In case of a lawsuit, your corporation's assets will be on the line and not your personal ones. The traditional corporation is a C corp. This company is owned by its shareholders and elects a board of directors that governs its policies. The board appoints a CEO to handle the day-to-day operations and also defines their compensation. In many corporations, the board of directors and the upper management of a company are the same people.

Taxation is a bit more complex in the case of corporations. They pay different tax rates than individuals. When the amount of profits you earn becomes large, corporate tax rates will result in you saving more money. However, all the money that you pay yourself from your corporation will incur income tax.

Formation

Forming a C corp is as straightforward as forming an LLC. However, given the implications of starting a corporation, it's preferable to hire the services of a qualified attorney who can help you with the process. You'll need to choose an available business name that complies with the naming rules of the state. Like with LLCs, you can incorporate a company in any state of your choice. You'll need to file Form SS-4 and file for an EIN, like with an LLC. Once this is done, the process diverges from that of an LLC's set up. You'll need to appoint directors and register your corporation by filing the articles of incorporation.

These articles are a bit different from an LLC's, and you should use a lawyer to draft this document. The filing fee ranges from $100 to $800 depending on the state you choose. You'll also need to identify the shareholders of the corporation and issue them stock. Only when this is done should you proceed to obtain all the necessary permits and licenses that I'll talk about in the next chapter.

Taxation

Taxation is a complex issue with regard to corporations. As I mentioned previously, corporations pay income taxes at different rates from individuals. The preparation of a corporation's tax return is a more involved process and isn't something you should undertake yourself. Corporations require almost constant accounting support since they'll need to pay estimated taxes to the IRS every month (Zaryzcki, 2020)/.

This means your books and statement of accounts have to be regularly updated and all your receipts entered into your accounting journals properly. Most LLC owners choose to track their taxes solo by using Quickbooks but corporation owners would be wise to hire the services of a CPA.Given their standalone entity status, corporations qualify for a range of tax credits that most individuals don't qualify for. you can also claim a larger range of tax deductions than are available to an LLC.

With corporate tax rates being lower than the individual rate, you could also lower your tax bill compared to what you would pay when running an LLC or a sole prop.

Advantages

There are many advantages to forming a corporation. The biggest one is the ability to raise capital. Raising capital from outside investors is extremely easy with a corporation since all you need to do is issue shares to them. Investors who wish to exit their investment can either sell their shares to another investor or sell them back to you. Shareholders receive a raft of protections under the laws of the United States and as a result, investor confidence is high. If you wish to raise debt (take a loan) from a bank, you'll find it easier to do than with an LLC. LLCs can raise money from banks but loan officers typically want to see a long track record of business. LLC owners are either small businesses or they're in an early stage of their business career. As a result, banks tend to view them as being risky.

Approach a bank as a corporation and you'll convey the impression of being a serious business person who has the capital they need to be able to run operations successfully.

Liability protection is an advantage I've already discussed. The duration of a corporation is unlimited which means passing ownership onto another person when you want to move on is easy. This isn't quite the case with LLCs where the company either has to be dissolved or complicated legal proceedings have to be initiated to pass ownership.

Disadvantages

Given the flexibility a corporation offers, it stands to reason that there are many clauses and bylaws that need defining before incorporation. For this reason, additional costs pile up when you want to incorporate. There are more regulations and paperwork to keep tabs on and you'll need to hire support staff to keep up with it. The other downside is that you could end up paying more taxes if you don't manage your withdrawal strategy well. This happens because you'll pay taxes at the company level and you'll then pay income taxes on the money you withdraw to your personal bank account. Most corporation owners choose to park money within their business so that the money can be reinvested. You need to carefully plan your approach in this regard.

S Corps

From the perspective of business structure, corporations are a solitary business entity. However, from a tax perspective, the IRS recognizes two types of corporations. The first is the C corp which you've just learned about. The second is an S corp. Double taxation is the difference between these two entities. S corps give their owners the ability to pass income through to their personal account and pay taxes just once on income.

There are restrictions on S corps that C corps don't have. First, S corps can have just 100 shareholders and they have to be US citizens. Usually, C corps can raise more capital by issuing different classes of stock. For example, one class might come attached with voting rights with the second class of stock might have a third of those rights. C corps are free to decide how they wish to distribute these rights.

S corps don't have this flexibility. They can issue just one class of stock and this limits their ability to raise capital. For this reason, S corps aren't suited for most business owners. If your aim is to withdraw as much capital from the business as possible as income, then choosing to be taxed as an S corp makes sense. If you aim to grow the business then a C corp is a much better structure. Note that forming an S corp is the same as a C corp. You'll need to file Form 2553 with the IRS to indicate that you wish to be taxed as an S corp. S corps attract greater scrutiny from the IRS due to the taxation arrangement. You'll need to make sure you follow all the relevant guidelines to remain an S corp. If the IRS decides you've violated them, you will get kicked back to C corp status automatically.

Double taxation and reducing your self-employment tax bill are the biggest advantages of choosing to operate as an S corp. The rules surrounding an S corp also vary by state so you should use the services of a professional before choosing to operate as one.

Which Structure Is Right for You?

There is an additional structure that I haven't covered as yet. It's a general partnership. A partnership works the same way as a sole prop does. It also comes with the same risks of a sole prop, and for this reason, it isn't a good fit for your trucking business. The best corporate structure is either an LLC or a C corp. Which one should you choose? If you're starting out and don't have large reserves of capital, an LLC is your best choice. You can always adapt it to fit your needs as your business grows. What qualifies as a "large" reserve of capital? Here's a simple rule of thumb. If you look at the capital you have and ask yourself whether it's large enough, it probably isn't. Stick with an LLC and grow your business in a safe and controlled manner.

Starting off as a trucking corporation (C corp) requires a lot of capital since the margins are small and you'll have to deal with lengthy credit cycles. If you work with freight brokers most of them will pay you on a net30 basis. If you work with customers/shippers directly, they'll pay you on a net60 or even 90 basis. You won't have much leverage with either party because you're their supplier and there might be more like you. This is why it's important to pick a good niche for yourself. I'll explain this later in the book.

For now, take a close look at each corporate structure and stick to an LLC if you have any doubts. When running your LLC make sure you separate your business and personal bank accounts right from the beginning. This will help establish the impression that you're conducting business separately. There have been instances where business owners did not separate their finances and ended up losing their liability protection in court. So always use a separate bank account to conduct business.

In terms of timelines, setting up an LLC or a corporation can be finished in as little as a week. If you use a service, you can set yourself up within a few days as well. However, you need to conduct proper research and use the services of the right professionals. Many business owners are used to doing things themselves and back themselves to figure things out. This is a great attitude to have. However, when it comes to running a successful trucking business, you have to focus on processes and empower people to do things for you. This means hiring out jobs that aren't in your primary area of expertise. Your accountant and attorney are going to be your best business friends since they'll literally save you money. Your accountant will help you locate tax credits that you can apply for and lower your tax bill while your attorney will help you craft foolproof agreements that will protect you no matter what. So don't skimp on these expenses when you set up your business. Speaking of support staff, you'll also need to hire a registered agent as I mentioned previously. These people can help you form a company as well. Registered agents figure mostly when you begin to apply for your licenses and other permits you'll need to run your business. Let's now take a look at all of those requirements and see how you can go about applying for them.

Chapter 3:
Licenses and Permits

If there's one constant about the logistics industry, it's that you need a permit to do anything. As a trucker, you'll be subject to a variety of laws aimed at increasing safety on the roads. These laws protect you as well as those around you. It's in your best interest to always adhere to them and not risk a fine. A fine or a transgression will destroy your reputation and could be terminal for your business. Each state has different rules regarding the permits you'll need to operate. It's impossible to dive into the minute requirements of every state but most of them adhere to a few basic principles. In this chapter, you'll be learning the most commonly applied rules. There are Federal rules you need to comply with as well. FMCSA or the Federal Motor Carrier Safety Administration is the regulatory body you'll need to pay attention to. Let's begin by looking at the steps involved in obtaining your permits.

Application Steps

Figuring out all of the things you need to do to get your business up and running and be difficult. There are a few steps that you'll need to carry out before you're allowed to operate a truck.

Briefly, here they are in order of execution (*License and Permit Checklist for Starting a Trucking Company*, 2020):

1. Get a commercial driver's license (CDL)
2. Apply for your DOT and MC numbers with FMCSA
3. Complete your Unified Carrier Registration (UCR)
4. Apply for and obtain an International Registration Plan tag (IRP)
5. Adhere to heavy use tax regulations
6. Obtain an International Fuel Tax Agreement (IFTA) decal
7. File a BOC-3
8. Obtain a Standard Carrier Alpha Code (SCAC)

Eight steps seem like a lot of trouble to go through to get the show on the road. However, most of these steps can be executed from a centralized system so it isn't as if you need to apply at multiple places. Execute these steps one by one and you'll get done with them in no time. The first step is to apply for a CDL. If you already have one, you can skip the next section. If not, read on!

Obtaining a CDL

Obtaining a CDL is the most important step in the process. After all, without a license you can't drive on the roads. The CDL application process is probably the lengthiest portion of the process I listed above. There are many elements to it such as medical requirements, residency requirements, and skills tests. The first step you should take is to get a copy of your state's Commercial Driver's Licensing manual. This manual is an important document since each state has its own process of applying for a CDL. Study this manual and it will list everything you need to know. The manual can be obtained at any DMV or from your state licensing department's website. The second step to take is to decide what kind of vehicle you'll be driving. "Truck" isn't a type of vehicle unfortunately. There are different categories of trucks and rigs and you should know which one you're going to use to run your business. Your choice of vehicle depends on your niche as well so make sure you read the chapters detailing this later in the book.

Some classes of license require special permits. Tractor trailers fall under this category so if a trailer happens to be a part of your vehicle, you'll need to keep this in mind. You'll have to pass a written and skills test no matter the kind of vehicle you're looking to drive. Once you've made these decisions, you'll need to complete two steps. The first is to obtain your CLP or Commercial Learner's Permit. This permit authorizes you to practice on public roads with a qualified CDL holder with you in the cab. Applying for the CLP requires you to show the authorities a bunch of paperwork that certifies you as being medically fit to drive a vehicle as well as knowledgeable enough. Here's where the CDL manual comes in handy.

Each state has different requirements. On a high level, there are three categories of documents you'll need to provide (*How do I get a Commercial Driver's License?* | *FMCSA*, 2020):

1. Identity and residence proof
2. Proof of adequate health (more on this in a bit)
3. Proof of knowledge (you'll need to pass a test after studying for it with the materials you'll be given)

The health requirements are what vary the most from one state to another. Some states require you to have a DOT medical card and pass a DOT approved physical. Getting a DOT medical card is quite straightforward. You'll need to inquire with the DMV about DOT approved medical practitioners in your area and schedule a physical with them.

The examiner will review your medical history and perform a check for diabetes or any harmful infections. Once the physical is finished, they'll submit a report to the National Registry of Certified Medical Examiners. You'll receive a copy of the Medical Examiner's certificate. This is your DOT card, in effect. The kinds of infections and diseases that you'll be screened for varies from one state to another. If you don't pass the physical, you can appeal the decision and consult another practitioner.

As far as identity and residence proof is concerned you can provide a copy of your personal driving license, identity card, or passport. You can provide a lease agreement or a utility bill to prove your residence address. Once these documents have been submitted, you can schedule a date to appear for your theoretical test and will have to pass it. Some of the questions on this test will seem like common sense but don't underestimate them. If you fail the test, you can retake it after a few days. Learning materials will either be provided to you or the CLD manual will let you know where you can obtain them.

These days most states have online repositories from which you can download and print learning material. Once you've obtained your CLP, you can begin practicing on the roads with someone who holds a registered CDL. If you don't know anyone who has one, you can enroll yourself in a driving school where you'll learn the right skills. It's best to enroll in a school instead of trying to wing it with your friend.

The CDL manual will list the skills you'll be tested on so make sure you study it well. Again, different states have different tests. What's universal is that you'll have to possess the CLP for at least 14 days before appearing for your skills test. There are three parts to the skills test:

1. Vehicle inspection
2. Basic controls
3. Road safety

Some states allow you to carry a checklist that can aid you in your vehicle inspection test. Either way you'll have to study hard and practice driving to pass the skills test. Note that a pass/fail decision is in the hands of the observer. If you follow rules to the T but are still driving in a less than intuitive or safe manner, the observer can fail you.

Once you've passed the test you can take all of your documents to the DMV for processing. Some states issue the CDL on the same day while some will send it to you in the mail to your residence address. Make sure your name and details are correct on the application forms. Do not use aliases or any fancy contortions of your name. Your CDL identity will carry over to everything else in the process. For example, if your name is Jane Smith, don't abbreviate your name to J. Smith, Janey Smith, JJ Smitty, or anything else you can think of. Periods in your name can alter the structure. For example, Jane.Smith and Jane Smith are different names. Remember that it is the state government that issues your CDL and not FMCSA. Any disputes or changes have to be filed with the state, not the federal government.

Obtaining a DOT and MC Number

I'd like to point out that you don't need to have formed a company to obtain a CDL. However, it's best to form a business structure before you obtain your DOT and MC numbers. You'll have to obtain them in the name of your company. Technically speaking, you can obtain it in your name and use it since you're an owner-operator. However, if you're involved in any incidents, your LLC will not protect you since it doesn't have the authority (license) to protect you. If you already have an MC and DOT numbers, you'll need to file another Form MCS-150 to get the name changed on the current number. Note that a change on the DOT number doesn't carry over to the MC number.

If you don't have an MC number, you'll begin by first applying for a DOT number. Back in the day, this meant having to visit two different offices but these days, there's a central system that you can use to apply for your authority. The link for the Unified Registration System is https://www.fmcsa.dot.gov/registration/fraudulent-and-misleading-marketing-new-fmcsa-applicants.

If you don't have a DOT number, you'll have to apply for one at the same link. This is a straightforward application and you'll typically receive a number within a few hours or two days at the most. Once you receive your DOT number, you'll have to log into the system again and apply for an FMCSA authority. There are two kinds of authorities you can apply for if you wish to move goods.

The first is a Motor Carrier of Property, except Household Goods and the second is Motor Carrier of Household Goods. Household goods are anything that is deemed of use within a residence or is slated for use within one. You'll have to file separately for both authorities and pay the fee of $300 each time. The form you'll fill out is the same, the OP-1.

Note that you cannot fill a physical form. Everything is done online these days. The exception is if you already possess an authority and want to add another one. Completing the Form OP-1 is the first step in receiving your authority. Here's how the process works:

1. Fill and submit OP-1 online
2. You're issued an MC number instantly (you can't operate under it as yet)
3. Simultaneous steps
   a. 10 day protest period commences
   b. Insurance company files relevant forms with FMCSA
   c. Process agent files BOC-3 with FMCSA
4. You'll receive the permit and certificate after previous step is complete

Let's look at the form OP-1 first. The first section requires you to acknowledge that you'll hire a process agent in every state you operate in. Remember that your registered agent when you form a company can act as a process agent as well. Make sure they're registered in every state you wish to do business in. Note that you'll have to hire a process agent even for states you transit through. For example, if you drive from Ohio to New York, via Pennsylvania you'll need a PA process agent.

Next, you'll enter your legal business name and indicate the kind of structure it is. If you're a sole prop for some reason, you can indicate your "doing business as" or DBA name in this section. You'll enter your principal office address. For most truckers, this is a confusing section to enter. You can simply enter the address of your registered agent. You'll have to enter a mailing address if it's different from the office address.

You'll then indicate the authority you're applying for. The third section of the form deals with insurance information and you'll have to enter all the details. There are two types of insurance you'll need to obtain. These are BI (bodily injury) and PD (property damage). FMCSA indicates the maximum coverage limits for each category. You'll need to obtain insurance that is equivalent to the highest limit in the boxes that you check. Each box corresponds to a gross vehicle weight. If you've applied for the carrier of household goods authority, you'll require coverage amounting to $750,000 of BI and Pd liability as a minimum. Section four of the form lists the safety certification requirements. If you're going to operate vehicles with a gross weight of less than 10,000 pounds, you're exempt from these regulations. If you're going to operate vehicles greater than 10,000 pounds in weight or carry hazardous materials, you must read and indicate that you understand all of the points. If you've applied for a carrier of household goods authority, you need to fill out section six of the form and indicate that you understand all of the statements in there. Lastly, in section 8 you need to certify that all information you've provided is true to your knowledge under penalty of perjury. This concludes the OP-1. Once you submit the form, the process I mentioned above begins. You'll be assigned an MC number, but you can't operate under it as yet. During the 10-day protest window, anyone who objects to your being appointed with an authority can list their objection with FMCSA. Receiving an objection is a pretty rare occurrence. Meanwhile, you need to contact a process agent and insurance broker to get your insurance and Form BOC-3 in place. Insurance coverage will be dictated by the amount of cover you want. At a minimum, you need to ensure you've covered for the amounts indicated in the OP-1. Shop for good brokers and don't settle on the one that simply offers the lowest premium. You'll be operating a heavy vehicle and the consequences of an incident can be huge. It's best to make sure you're covered as much as possible. Process agents will begin to get in touch with you the moment you're assigned an MC number. This is because FMCSA publicizes your appointment and process agents have access to your database. Pick a process agent that is experienced in handling legal matters and has a large footprint. Ask for references and the MC numbers of those references. You want someone who responds to your questions quickly and has a large national footprint. This will remove the need for you to register yourself in every state you will drive through.

Your insurance broker and process agent will file all necessary paperwork with FMCSA and once the protest period ends, you'll be mailed your authority. Once you receive this, you're officially ready to conduct business.

Complete the Unified Carrier Registration

The UCR program is a federally mandated system that registers operators of commercial motor vehicles involved in interstate or international travel. It's an annual filing that must be renewed by the end of each year.

If you're operating a commercial vehicle of any kind that crosses state lines, you need to register with the system. The greater the number of vehicles in your fleet, the higher your registration fee is. Penalties for not filing a UCR is detainment of your vehicle and additional fines of up to $5,000.

The UCR filing has been a source of confusion because only 41 of the 50 states participate in it. If you belong to one of the states below, you don't have to register. Note that non-participation is determined by your state of residence, not the state of legal filing:

- Arizona
- Florida
- Hawaii
- Maryland
- Nevada
- New Jersey
- Oregon
- Vermont
- Wyoming
- District of Columbia

The process of applying for a UCR is extremely straightforward. You'll need to visit https://www.ucr.gov and register using your MC number and provide vehicle details. The fee for operates running less than two trucks is $59 per year.

Obtain an International Registration Plan (IRP) Tag

The IRP tag is something that is specific to your home state. Each state has different requirements. It's best to visit https://www.fmcsa.dot.gov/international-programs/canada/international-registration-plan-irp and click on your home state to review the requirements. The IRP tag allows you to operate your vehicle across state lines and even in Canadian provinces. If you're going to be driving across state lines, it's imperative that you apply for this tag.

The rules are listed on each state's DMV website. Alternatively, you can visit the offices of the DMV to obtain information on how you receive the tag. You'll need copies of your CDL and MC number authority to complete the process.

Again, this is a very simple process and you can expect your tags within a few days or even a few hours in some states.

Review Heavy Use Tax Rules

Trucks that weigh more than 55,000 pounds are subject to heavy use taxes. The IRS will require you to file Form 2290 with your year-end tax returns.

This filing is quite straightforward and it depends on how much mileage you've clocked over the year. You can hire an accountant to file this for you but it's best to visit the IRS website at www.irs.gov to understand how the regulations work.

Obtain an IFTA Decal

The International Fuel Tax Agreement decal is yet another DMV controlled process. The IFTA was introduced to simplify fuel usage reporting by heavy trucks across the United States. Your company will have a single fuel license and you'll need to report your fuel usage to the DMV every quarter.

Each state's DMV has a different process. In California, for example, you need to file everything online, but some states still rely on manual processes.

Check with your local DMV as to how you can go about filing this paperwork.

Filing the BOC-3 Form

This form will be filed by your process agent so you don't have to worry about this. If your process agent doesn't file it within the 10-day period, get yourself a new agent and have them file it. There are no penalties for not filing the form within this period. It's just that you want to hire an agent that is efficient.

Obtain a Standard Carrier Alpha Code

SCAC codes don't have anything to do with the government and are actually controlled by the National Motor Freight Traffic Association. If you plan on hauling military, government, international, or intermodal loads, you'll need an SCAC code. You can apply for a code at https://secure.nmfta.org/New/NewApplicationPrivacy.aspx?r=637 8C37EEFD09DF46811. You'll have to pay $93 to obtain this code. Note that you'll need to review this code every year by June 30th.This concludes our look at the permits and licenses you'll need. As you can see, the lengthiest application is the FMCSA MC number. Everything else is a straightforward form that can be filled online without any waiting periods. In the larger scheme of things, the FMCSA authority fee is the highest at $300. Every other filing comes in under $100 and isn't exorbitant. FMCSA publishes detailed guides for filling out the OP-1 that you can obtain at the links mentioned previously.

I haven't spoken about equipment as yet. It's now time to take a look at that vital part of your business.

Chapter 4:
Buying or Leasing the Right Equipment

There are so many trucks and types of equipment out there for truckers these days. Almost every product is great, and truth be told, it's close to impossible to make a terrible choice. However, as an owner-operator you need to figure out a few things that the average driver doesn't need to contend with. For starters, you're working on your own time and every second your truck spends in the shop or waiting for spare parts is losing you money. Drivers get compensated for service issues, but you won't. For this reason, choosing the right equipment is crucial. The choice often comes down to seemingly small issues, but they make a huge difference. Before diving into the right kind of vehicle for your needs, let's take some time to understand how you can make your choice easier. For starters, what is your niche? Are you looking to move specialized loads such as cold chain products or HAZMAT? In this case, you'll have to spend more time researching your equipment and their safety characteristics. The cost of this equipment will be greater than the average semi as well. However, these loads pay more. The distance of your routes is also another way to niche yourself. Are you looking to go local, short-haul, or long-haul? This choice dictates the size of the trailer you need and the specs on the equipment. Take some time to think about this choice.

I'll address the niche question later in this book when I'll show you how to market yourself and find the best paying loads. For now, let's move on and look at the best make of truck you can choose.

How to Pick the Best Truck

I'll start off by saying that there is no one size fits all truck. Everyone's different and your preferences won't be the same as mine. Your niche will also dictate what kind of truck makes the most sense for you. The choice of truck brand is a contentious one. Some truckers swear by Kenworth while others think Volvos are the best thing since sliced bread. Your equipment is going to be very close to you as you run your business so it shouldn't come as a surprise that truckers are passionate about them. Your first truck is a critical decision so don't take it lightly. Here are some pertinent questions to answer that will help you make a good choice.

What Kind of Routes Are You Hauling?

Your choice of truck depends on the distance you'll be traveling in it. For local routes you'll probably want something that is fuel-efficient and maneuvers easily. Your truck will also be smaller than some of the long-haul trucks. Long haul equipment needs to be comfortable above all else. Fuel economy is an important factor but sacrificing it for comfort makes no sense.

Most long-haul trucks react to driver input very differently from trucks suited for local hauls. The long-haul trucks tend to work better at higher speed and are designed to cruise on the interstate. Short-haul trucks fall somewhere in between. You might want a sleeper cab in one but depending on the way your structure your hours, you might not need one. It comes down to personal preference.

Cab Style

If you choose short or local hauls you can get away with choosing a day cab truck. These trucks are pretty basic in terms of amenities and are less spacious inside than long haul trucks. Even within long haul trucks, there are different varieties of cabs you'll find. Some cabs are ultra-luxurious featuring beds that would put a hotel room to shame. Almost all of them have kitchen areas and are designed for long haul comfort.

Fuel Economy

This is a big one. you want your truck to be fuel efficient no matter what. However, the haul distance often dictates truck design.

For example, most short-haul trucks have conventional noses that project outward at an almost 90-degree angle. This makes it very easy to reach the engine and conduct maintenance. However, fuel economy suffers since the shape isn't aerodynamic. Long haul trucks are usually slope nosed. This makes maintenance tougher to carry out but they're extremely fuel efficient. There's also the roof to take into account. Some trucks have a raised roof that accommodates a sleeping bunk, while some have larger cabs and a mid-roof. The mid-roof is more aerodynamic and saves fuel. However, you can haul bigger loads with a raised roof. Don't overthink this too much. If you're driving short-hauls, your fuel economy is going to be poor since you'll encounter more traffic than the average long hauler. Choose a truck that is easy to maintain and has a decent fuel economy. If you're long hauling, go with a good level of comfort and then figure out how you can squeeze fuel economy into the equation.

Are You Paying Cash or Financing?

Your truck will be the biggest investment and asset in your business. Buying a used truck can be a good decision financially but if it doesn't allow you to haul loads, it isn't really worth it. You might also end up spending more on maintenance than you bargained for. For this reason, it's important to consider the option of financing your truck. I'll explain everything to do with financing later in this chapter.

The costs of semi-trucks vary quite a lot. A standard truck with a day cab can start from $80,000 while a new long haul with a deluxe sleeper cab can run as much as $150,000. If you opt for luxury options, you can add another $50,000 to this price. Used truck prices depend on their mileage. A brand new semi is built to last a million miles. You can find good used trucks for $30,000. Trucks that need some work can sell for as little as $10,000.

Bad Weather Handling

This factor is especially important if you're going to long haul loads. You will encounter bad weather at some point, and you need a truck that handles well.

This isn't just a question of preference, it's about safety as well. Bad weather is one of the leading causes of accidents on the highways and the last thing you want is to find yourself embroiled in a lawsuit. That will end your business faster than choosing the wrong truck. The best way to gather bad weather handling performance feedback is to talk to other truckers. You can also visit Facebook groups such as Trucker

Feed and Trucker Haven and network with truckers on there to get their opinions. Remember that everyone is extremely attached to their equipment so take everything they say with a grain of salt. However, pay attention to the examples they provide of poor weather handling.

Dealership Network

Unlike cars or smaller vehicles that can be serviced by smaller mechanics, truck operators rely on their dealership network. Sure, you can find a few mechanics in a truck stop, but this isn't a scalable solution. Your dealer plays a bigger role in your choice of truck than with your regular vehicle. First, you need to evaluate their network. How many locations do they have and what is their reputation?

Check online sources such as Trustpilot or Facebook groups for reviews of truck dealerships. Some dealerships have a reputation of being tough to get into. International manufacturers such as Volvo are notorious for this. Almost every spare part has to be flown in from Europe and this can take up to a week. Many truckers who find themselves in an emergency situation end up customizing a solution for themselves from a local mechanic. This can compromise your safety so it's an unacceptable solution. Some of the more popular brands of trucks have a large number of dealerships but they can be tough to get into. Due to their popularity, their shops are always full and this can hamper your business.

Freightliner is a good example of a dealer network that is extremely busy despite having many locations throughout the country. Kenworth and Peterbilt have good dealer networks and as of this writing, aren't too busy to hamper servicing.

Ride Quality

You'll be spending most of your time in your truck, so ride quality is essential. You don't want to be bouncing around like a bobblehead doll on a long haul. Short-haul and local trucks might not travel very far but you don't want to settle for poor ride quality.

The best sources for gathering feedback on trucks are the Facebook groups mentioned previously. So, having got all of that out of the way, let's now look at the best trucks for different routes.

Best Truck Makes

When looking at short-haul trucks you want them to be mechanically sound. This means the brand isn't as important. Stick to makes that have a good reputation for being well built. The freightliner is a popular option in the short-haul market. Paccar is also a popular option. Freightliners are less expensive and are lighter in weight as well. If your niche happens to be construction or if you're undertaking dump truck work, then Western Star or Mack are good options. They're heavier trucks which makes them ill-suited for long-hauls, but their sturdy frames mean they'll last for a long time over short-hauls. Volvos are a great choice but always buy them used. This is because the market is flooded with used Volvos. Big carriers buy them en masse and then discard them after a few years' use. This means you can score a great truck at decent prices. A word of caution here.

Remember that Volvos will have spare part issues. This is why it's best to use them for short-hauls. Another brand that often comes up is International. However, these trucks haven't met emissions standards yet so they might not be the best choice.

All of these recommended makes will do well in local routes as well. You can opt for used options since it'll be easier for you to access a dealership and get the truck serviced.

Best Long-Haul Trucks

You want long haul trucks to be comfortable, smooth, and to handle well in bad weather. An extensive dealership network is non-negotiable. To this end Kenworth and Peterbilt are excellent makes. Freightliners aren't always the best for long hauls but some of their models are well suited for it.

It's a personal choice at the end of the day. Paccar is perhaps the best make for long haul trucks. Do your research and make sure you visit multiple dealerships before settling on a truck.

You want to test out as many trucks as possible. Negotiate hard and compare prices online. You can use websites such as Arrow Truck Sales,

Trucker to Trucker, My Little Salesman, and Commercial Truck Trader to compare prices. You'll find many options amongst used trucks so let's look at how you can evaluate these trucks.

Evaluating a Used Truck

Evaluating a used truck is as simple as following a few steps. First, check the maintenance logs and the hours logs. This will tell you exactly how well the truck was maintained and how long it was driven. Pay special attention to when the tires were changed. Often, tires will be changed at different times so their mileage will vary. Ideally, all tires will be replaced at the same time. If your seller doesn't have logs, then don't bother. When evaluating the trailer, look for rust. You cannot store loads safely when rust is present. Look at the trailer during daylight hours. Rust often appears as raised spots under the surface and can be easy to miss.

Make sure you inspect everything thoroughly. Take a look at the windows and doors to make sure they're sealed properly. Leaky windows will reduce your fuel mileage and will slow you down. During bad weather, your cab will be a very uncomfortable place with a leaky door. Tires are a big part of any truck. Check the treads to make sure they haven't disappeared. Aside from this, check for any signs of a bent hubcap or cracks on them. These are signs of overloading or underinflated tires or parking in wet areas.

Wet areas damage the suspension, and this will increase your maintenance bill. Make sure all the tires are from the same manufacturer. If not, ask the seller why this is the case. The engine is the heart of the truck. It shouldn't have any leaks, smoke, dirt, rust, poorly connected cables, or make odd noises when switched on. Rev it a few times to make sure everything works well. Oil leaks are common on old trucks. A well-maintained truck won't have these issues. Check the filter for the cleanliness of the oil. Semis hold over 15 gallons of the stuff, so you want to make sure it's clean. The brakes must not have any rust or corrosion. All the lights on the truck should be functional.

Make sure they work as intended. If they don't, you'll be hit with costly traffic fines. The seat is an important part of the overall driving experience. Used truck seats can get a bit dented over time, with the cushion moving around. Make sure you sit in it for some time and pay attention to how your back feels. This is where stress will hit you over long hauls so paying attention to it upfront is a good idea.

Lastly, speak to the seller and ask them for the reason they're selling their truck. Don't be rude but you do want to be assertive. It's a good idea to ask them the same question in multiple ways and check to see if their answers are consistent. Any inconsistencies indicate situations that need further digging.

Make sure you research the standard features on the truck before you visit the seller. Here are some of the most common ones on trucks:

- Drag reducing fairings - These plastic fixtures are attached to the sides of the truck and reduce drag on highways
- Skirts - These appendages reduce wind resistance under the trailer and reduce turbulence. The result is a smoother ride.
- Tires - Wide tires improve handling but can reduce speed. Low-roll resistance tires require less energy to turn but their grip might not be the best in harsh weather.
- Aluminum hubs - These wheels reduce the strain on the axles and will allow you to carry heavier loads.

- Mudflaps - Flaps play an important role in decreasing wind resistance and increasing fuel efficiency.
- Transmissions - These days all transmissions are controlled by computers. Some new trucks have sensors that monitor everything from your state to that of the components of the truck.

Whether you're buying used or new, you have the choice of paying in cash or via financing. Financing a semi isn't as straightforward as financing a regular vehicle. Let's look at how it works next.

How to Finance Your Truck

Rigs can get expensive. Depending on the kind of equipment you're looking for and on the type of horsepower you want from your truck, you're looking at a cost of over $100,000. This isn't small money. If you happen to have that much cash lying around then feel free to buy a truck using the guide in the first half of this chapter. However, most folks need to obtain some form of financing.

There are three broad ways you can go about obtaining financing for your truck. The first is to opt for carrier financing. These programs are also called lease owner-operator programs and are a terrible deal for a driver. I'll shortly explain why. The other two options you have are to opt for a traditional loan or a lease. Let's begin by looking at why you need to stay away from lease owner-operator plans.

Why Lease Owner Operator Plans Are a Bad Choice

Lease owner-operator plans have been around the trucking industry for a long time. As the cost of owning a rig increases and as the demand for drivers increases, more of these plans have cropped up. This doesn't mean they're a good choice though. A trucking lease operator is a driver who bears all the costs of being an owner-operator. You'll have to pay the costs of leasing the truck, fuel, maintenance, taxes, etc., while the trucking company owns the title to the truck. These programs seem attractive because there's usually no money down or very little down payment required. Sounds good so far, doesn't it? However, there's a lot going on underneath the surface. For starters, the carrier is fully in charge. They structure the lease agreement to favor them in every situation. The first clause in this agreement typically binds you to the carrier and forbids you from hauling loads for anyone else, even if it is for your own company. This means if you don't receive enough miles in a month, you'll end up owing the carrier money for your truck. This payment covers just the lease. You'll still have to pay for fuel and everything else related to the maintenance of the truck. Thus, you're neither an owner-operator who can choose their loads, nor are you an employee who can count on a steady salary and benefits. You get the worst of both worlds. The other issue with these programs is that the trucks you're leased might be pieces of junk. The carrier is the one that selects your truck for you and the driver has no say in the process. You might end up paying a high cost per month to lease a piece of rubbish that requires constant maintenance. This only increases your cost per month. Anecdotal evidence suggests that lease operators often end up owing the carrier money at the end of the month. Typically, beginner drivers without the cash to finance a truck fall for these programs. However, they're designed to bleed you dry so never make the mistake of signing up for them. Increasingly, CDL training schools have also begun offering these programs. They might be branded as a "freedom" plan or as a "never never" plan. Never-never simply means you should never ever opt for these plans. All of these programs give you the option of owning the truck at the end of the lease period. Many lease operators think this is what makes the deal worthwhile. They think they'll work under a lease for two or three years and put up with the carrier's conditions. After all, they get to own the truck at the end of the period. However, there are catches here as well. First off, you need to pay the carrier a lump sum to own the truck. This is almost always greater than $20,000. You'll be losing money for three years just to pay the carrier even more money to own your rig. Besides, the total expense of buying the truck adds up to far more than what the rig will be worth after depreciation. You'll be leased a used truck almost always. Let's say the value of this truck is $70,000. Assuming your lease term is three years and you pay $600 every month to the carrier, you'll end up paying (36*600) $21,600 for the truck over this period. This doesn't include other costs of ownership like insurance and maintenance. At the end of the three-year period, your buyout payment will amount to $30,000 or more on a truck that initially costs $70,000. Except, your truck won't be worth that much at the end of the period. It will depreciate in value. Truck depreciation is usually at its highest in the first two years. This means you can expect your truck to be worth half its value when you reach the end of your lease period. Going back to our example, this means you'll pay over $50,000 for a truck that is worth around $45,000. These are rough numbers, but it happens quite often. The other disadvantage is that you can't claim any of the tax deductions associated with owning a truck. One of the biggest tax deductions you can take is depreciation on your truck. However, in this arrangement you don't own the truck and can't claim it. So not only are you making less money, you're paying high taxes on the money you do manage to make. Your success at the end of the day depends on the trucking company. If they aren't on your side, you have almost no shot at succeeding. It's of zero assurance that the average company that offers these kinds of programs isn't trustworthy. Experienced truckers have heard of outfits such as Midwestern Distribution, C.R. England, and Prime Leasing. These companies were and are prolific lease operators and have all suffered legal action or government-enforced shutdowns due to shady practices. It's far better to work as an owner-operator. It's just better business. You'll be in full control of your equipment and your loads. You can choose higher paying jobs instead of being forced to fight for whatever scraps the carrier throws your way. Understand that the lease operating agreement doesn't create any losses for the carrier. You bear everything and need to figure out how you can make money. Most people don't. If you haul loads for another carrier, you'll be penalized or have your contract terminated. This means the payments you've made previously are for nothing. In short, it's a losing proposition for you. Instead, seek to finance your truck via a loan or through a standard leasing agreement with a dealer.

Loans for Truck Drivers and Operators

I'll be upfront with you: It's tough to qualify for a loan to finance a truck purchase. Most lenders are wary of giving cash to new truck owners and the rates on new trucks can be massive. Even used trucks are seen as risky by the banks so it can be tough to get the cash you need. However, this doesn't mean it's impossible.

These days there are many online lenders such as Stilt and Kabbage who provide truck drivers with loans of up to $250,000 which can be put towards a truck purchase. There are a few boxes you must tick though.

For starters, every lender is going to want to figure out whether you can actually repay the loan. The way they do this is to evaluate your income to check whether it meets the lender's minimum requirements. Lenders calculate what's called a back ratio or a debt to income ratio. They divide all of your monthly debt payments (credit card, mortgage, personal vehicle debt) by your income. If this number comes in under 36%, it's a good start. Lenders will also want to check your experience in the business. This is where new applicants lose out. If you're starting out as an owner-operator, you won't have any experience running a business even if you've been driving a rig for many years. They'll want to see official documents that prove your work history and employment. If you don't have a substantial history, then do your best to show them you're competent. Your credit history is also a very important part of your application.

If your credit score is greater than 640, you can expect to be treated favorably by the lender. Anything less than this pretty much kills your chances of scoring a loan, even if the other portions of your application are great. Lenders can exercise discretion but at the end of the day, most of them are unlikely to overlook a poor credit score.

Some lenders offer secured loans if your application is borderline acceptable. With these loans, you'll have to post collateral with the lender, and this is typically not a good idea. You'll be posting an asset as collateral to secure something that is decreasing in value. Unless the lender accepts some other form of collateral, don't opt for this. Other options to avoid are payday loans and "bad credit" loans. Both of these options offer extremely high interest rates. For that money, you can lease a better truck. Besides, both of these types of lenders will hold the title of your truck. If you fail to repay the loan your truck will be repossessed. Since qualifying for a truck loan is so difficult, the government offers a few programs that you can use.

The National Clean Diesel Funding Assistance program will provide you with all the help you need if you're looking to start a new business. You can visit their website at http://business.edf.org/projects/national-clean-diesel-funding-assistance-program. The U.S Small Business Administration also offers great funding options for small business owners. You can visit them at https://www.sba.gov/ to learn more. If you do qualify for a loan, remember to account for additional fees such as appraisal fees, application fees, and credit check fees. It's best to ask for a fee schedule from your lender before applying for a loan. This way you'll be going in with both eyes open.

Leases

There are two kinds of leases you can opt for when looking to finance your truck. The first is a capital or finance lease and the second is an operating lease. A capital lease is a less common variant, but it might be more beneficial for owner-operators. Capital leases are essentially loans that go towards your truck. The difference is that the monthly payments are usually lower than what you can expect on a traditional loan and there is a balloon payment at the end that you'll need to make to buy the truck.

All capital lease payments are structured to reduce the balloon payment amount to less than $100 so it's not like a lease owner-operator deal where you'll be squeezed for money. In fact, capital lease terms state that your balloon payment will reflect less than the fair market value of the truck. The deal is in your favor and isn't loaded against you.

The financing term ranges from 36 to 60 months. Longer terms are available, but it doesn't make sense to finance your truck for that long. Best of all, you get to keep the title and the truck is an asset in your business. In accounting terms, this means you get to depreciate it and claim that amount as a tax deduction on your annual return. What's more, the monthly payment you make can also be deducted as interest expense, further lowering your tax bill.

The monthly payments you make will cover around 90% of the truck's value. You'll have to pay around 10% down when signing the deal. In practical terms, if you're financing a $70,000 truck, you'll have to pay $7,000 down and the remaining $63,000 will be split over your lease term. If you opt for a 60-month term (five years), you'll pay around $1,050 per month. This sounds like a lot but remember that you can deduct this amount from your earnings and save money.

Depreciation and deducting interest expenses are the two biggest advantages a capital lease gives you. There really aren't any disadvantages to this option.

The downpayment might be a bit steep for some but if you can't afford this amount, it's a good sign that you need to perhaps save more money and then try your hand at business. Note that some leases stipulate maximum mileage limits on trucks. Make sure you read the terms and conditions carefully before signing the deal.

The second financing option is an operating lease. This option is akin to renting your truck. You'll pay a monthly fee to the leasing company and you get to use your truck. There isn't any downpayment you'll need to pay. This makes an operating lease a great option for fleet operators who can instantly build a vast fleet for a fraction of the price.

The problem is that you're completely tied to the monthly fee payment. If you default on this payment your truck will be taken back by the leasing company and you'll be left without a vehicle. This is not the case with a capital lease. If you face short-term cash flow troubles, which are common in this business, you'll face the potential loss of your truck which will only put you further in a hole.

The other disadvantage is that you don't own the truck. It stays off your balance sheet and you don't get to claim depreciation expense. You can deduct the monthly payment as an operating expense, but this is a smaller deduction than depreciation. Like with capital leases, your monthly payments will pay for 90% of the value of the truck.

While the operating lease model has its disadvantages, there are some advantages as well. The biggest one is that it allows you to start up almost immediately.

Your taxes are also simplified since you don't need to account for depreciation. If you're looking to transition to becoming a fleet owner, you can replace your equipment quickly without having to worry about downtime.

Owner-operators will find a capital lease suits their needs better than an operating lease. However, take the time to speak to your dealer to understand the terms they're offering.

Applying for Leasing

You've learned of the options you have to finance your truck but how do you go about applying for leases? Many first-time business owners rush into the application process without taking the time to prepare beforehand.

This leads to rejected applications and frustration. Take some time to prepare your application and gather all the documents you'll need. This will save you a lot of energy.

Know Your Credit

The first step to take is to order your credit report from an online service. If you have a credit card, you're entitled to a free credit report every year. Note that your credit report will not list your credit score. Instead, it will list all of the unpaid (and paid) balances you have on your record. Review your credit report thoroughly to make sure there aren't any mistakes in there.

Often, old accounts don't get closed once paid off or erroneous balances might show up. Contact the ratings agencies to get these errors sorted out. Your credit report will list phone numbers you can call or online links you can use to file change requests. Make sure your credit is up to scratch before moving into the application process. Your credit score is a reflection of your credit report. If there's any outstanding debt you can clear before applying for a lease, do so.

Make sure your credit score is as high as it can possibly be so that you receive favorable terms. Next, you'll need a business plan to prove that you know what you're doing. I'll be walking you through creating a business plan later in this book so don't worry about this for now.

Briefly, your plan will need to demonstrate that you have a clear plan that will allow you to generate cash and secure work. You need to conduct an in-depth market analysis of your competition and your clients and project your cash flow into the future. This sounds like an extremely complicated thing to do but don't worry about this for now, I'll walk you through everything step by step later in this book.

Make sure your income taxes are paid in full and that your situation is stable. Unpaid taxes can result in disqualifications. Settle all of your debts (if any) with the IRS before starting a new business. If needed, approach a qualified accountant and check what you can do about your situation (if you have any issues.)

Prepare and Apply

The next step is to prepare all of your financial documents. You'll need to register your business before you continue, if you haven't done so already. Choose the right business structure for yourself. This is typically an LLC for most owner-operators as I've already explained. You will also need to supply some additional information such as the number of trucks you're looking to finance, your financial information such as your bank statements, previous income tax returns, and so on. You should also have a copy of your business plan with you.

The financing company will provide you with an application to fill out and they'll gather all of your documents. In most leasing companies, the person who you interact with will not be the one making the approval decision. This person, called the underwriter, sits behind closed doors and you'll never see them. Nor will they know who you are.

All they'll do is look at the numbers as dispassionately as possible. They might request further information from you to complete your application. If you receive a rejection, don't take it out on the person you interact with.

That person is usually on your side since they'll receive a commission for a successful application. Don't take rejection personally. Leasing companies are their own businesses and often, approval is based on their own books rather than having anything to do with you.

These companies go through cycles of approval and rejection. They might have financed too many long-haul trucks and are looking for smaller loads at the moment.

Or they could have an excess of short-hauls on their books and are looking to offload some longer haul equipment. From your perspective, apply to as many companies as possible and compare their rates and terms. Once your application is approved, carefully read through the terms they're offering you.

This will include the lease structure, the monthly payment, the term of your lease, and the interest rate. It's best to send this paperwork to an accountant you trust and have them review it for you. If you've prepared well in advance and have everything in order, you can receive approval in as little as 24 hours.

Usually, it takes around a week to complete everything. Something to note is that you will need to purchase disability insurance that can cover your monthly payments in case you suffer a disability or an injury that prevents you from working.

I'll discuss this in more detail in the chapter on insurance. However, approval is usually contingent on your obtaining disability insurance before you can take possession of your rig.

Dealing with Issues

Not everyone has great credit. Life happens to all of us and you might have suffered from adverse credit events or even bankruptcy in the past. Do these events mean you can never become an owner-operator?

Not quite. For starters, if you've suffered bankruptcy, you can apply for financing once you've been discharged from it. Your credit report will carry the record for a period of seven years. If you're approaching the seven-year limit on a previous bankruptcy, consider delaying your application until this period passes. If this limit is too far away, you can use a co-signer to help you bear the risk.

Usually, this person will be a trusted friend or family member. Your final option should be to post clear assets to function as collateral to secure the loan. The trucking business is a tough one and cash flow can be variable. Many leasing companies have options that allow you to switch your payment schedule.

For example, if your loads are seasonal, you might be offered an on and off plan where you pay for six months and don't pay for another six. Remember that everything on your lease agreement is negotiable. So negotiate! The down payment is also fully negotiable. Most lenders will want somewhere between 10-30% down. However, they will be willing to lower this rate if your credit score justifies a lower down payment or if you have prior experience in the business. Another negotiable option is to affix the kind of truck you'll be approved for. They might lease you an older truck that covers their risk and still satisfies your needs. Often lease terms will specify which dealers you can purchase from and will prevent you from buying a truck from a private sale. Other requirements might be stipulated as well. Remember, all of this is negotiable so make sure you negotiate well.

Make sure your truck has no incumbent liens on it since you don't want it to be repossessed by the primary creditor. If you're looking at used trucks, make sure it has less than 700,000 miles on it and is less than 10 years old. All of this seems like a lot to remember.

However, your truck is the biggest asset in your business, and you should spend a lot of time thinking about what kind of equipment you want and how you're going to go about financing it. A new truck will last longer, and you can find better financing deals on it, but don't discount used trucks as your monthly payments will be lower.

However, make sure you conduct a thorough examination of the vehicle before deciding to buy it. Use the guide earlier in this chapter to evaluate used trucks.

Other Equipment You'll Need

You're going to be spending a lot of time in your truck. At times it'll seem as if your truck is your real home instead of your physical house. You need to keep yourself as safe and comfortable as possible in there. There are many personal items that truck drivers bring along but here are some universal ones that you should always have with you.

Sunglasses

Sunglasses are the one piece of equipment that new drivers almost never bring along. It's easy to underestimate the effects of prolonged exposure to the sun will have on your eyes. Your driving abilities will naturally decrease, and you will feel far more fatigued than usual. Sunglasses are essential to keep you from having headaches or straining your eyes in bright sunshine. Shades break or get lost easily so buy more than one to keep your eyes safe. Don't be a scrooge when buying shades as well. Invest in high-quality glasses that wrap around your eyes and have a good degree of UV protection. It's also a good idea to affix them to a strap so that you don't have to worry about them falling to the ground and getting damaged.

Flashlight

Sunlight poses a problem for drivers as does no light. Night times can be tough to drive if you aren't experienced. Many long-time truckers prefer to drive at night because of cooler temperatures and lesser traffic. However, night driving brings its own challenges. A breakdown at night is just about the worst nightmare you can have. In such times, a flashlight pays major dividends. There are different kinds of flashlights available.

Truckers usually prefer a shake light, but any flashlight will do the trick. You can also buy a headlamp that will allow you to carry out emergency repairs in case of a breakdown while freeing your hands.

Make sure you have enough batteries of the right type in your rig so that you're always safe. Flashlights are also useful if you find yourself in an isolated area. There are many such spaces and a flashlight will discourage nefarious activity.

Backup Phone

As a trucker, you should have at least two phones at all times. Smartphones are a part and parcel of our lives these days. The thing about smartphones is that they're fragile and require constant charging. This makes traveling with them a problem. Some brand name phones are also finicky when they get older and mysteriously drop in performance. All of this adds up to an unreliable experience. Truck drivers these days use a variety of apps that help them do their job. You'll need a scanning app to send documents for verification, a camera to take pictures for evidence, and other apps to track your fuel usage and to track any rest stops along the way. This means you need to have a backup phone that has the same capabilities as your primary phone. Having separate phones for business and personal contacts is also a good idea. This will help you separate both sides of your life and will help you leave your work in your truck when you get home. Either way, make sure you have enough charging cables in your truck to keep your phone constantly charged. You can also buy a powerbank to power your phones in case of an emergency where you don't have access to a wall outlet.

Swiss Knife

Utility knives are a great survival tool and truck drivers carry them around for a reason. They're extremely useful when you want to carry out some emergency task like cutting twine from a haul or taking tire tread depth measurements. You can also use a knife for other odd tasks that come up every now and then.

GPS

GPS will be your constant companion when you're on the road. I must point out that GPS navigation systems designed for truck drivers are different from the ones that are designed for everyday road use. Make sure your device is designed specifically for a truck on the road and has maps that are regularly updated.

Your maps should take construction, traffic jams, road closures, and any other delay into account.

Work Gloves

Modern rigs are extremely comfortable to drive and sit in. However, our bodies aren't designed to be seated for long hours. You can't start walking around your cab when you're driving so you need as many creature comforts in your cab as possible. Most truck drivers ignore their hands and palms since they don't think about them as much as their backs and eyes.

Your hands can get tired gripping the wheel all day long and it's easy to scar and hurt your palms. Bring a pair of work gloves with you to protect your palms. They'll also come in handy if you want to fix something on your truck if something goes wrong. Cowboy gloves are a good option as well. They'll make your work easier and protect your hands.

Tools

Tools and a good toolbox are vital for on-road maintenance. Things will always go wrong when you're on the road and they have a tendency to do so at the worst moment possible. There are many categories of tools you'll need. The most basic one is a mallet and hammer. Trucks are sturdy things and you'll need these two to hammer nuts and bolts into place.

They can also be used in conjunction with other tools. Adjustable and oil filter spanners are also good to have in your rig. Socket spanners are also an excellent addition to your toolkit. If you're driving long haul, make sure you have both metric and US spanner sets.

This will help you avoid any headaches with international truck brands. Every rig has a number of complex systems within it. Despite the high-quality engineering you can expect from them, things tend to go wrong every now and then. Having a full kit of spare parts is essential to avoid a costly breakdown in the middle of nowhere. The items that usually have trouble are air and fuel lines, bulbs, and fuses. You should also carry antifreeze, a liquid wrench, and brake fluid to help you avoid any problems with those parts.

Cash

You don't want to carry too much cash with you since you'll find yourself in less than savory places now and then. However, you want to carry enough so that you're never short of resources. You won't have ready access to an ATM so carrying a few hundred dollars in cash is handy.

Water

Do you know that water doesn't cost the same everywhere? If you don't, you'll find out on a long haul soon enough! It's better to carry a large pack of bottled water with you before you set out instead of having to stop every 100 miles or so for a bottle of water. It's important to stay properly hydrated when driving. Many accidents are caused by drivers ignoring hydration when driving and losing concentration. Truck cabs are cool places and it can be easy to forget that you need to drink water. Avoid any issues and always keep lots of bottled water in your cab.

Slow Cooker

This is something many truck drivers don't have in their cabs but it's a great addition. Driving on the road often means you'll miss out on delicious, home-cooked meals. Slow cookers solve that issue. You can simply throw some ingredients into it and let it simmer away safely while you go about your job. In a few hours, you'll have a delicious meal. This will help you eat healthily and avoid having to wait to pass through a place you usually like to eat at. You can eat whenever you want, and this will make driving a more enjoyable experience. Now that we've covered equipment basics, it's time to look at the kind of insurance you'll need to run your business safely.

Chapter 5:
Getting the Right Insurance

Every successful business needs protection. Insurance policies offer this protection and have to be tailored for the business' unique needs. Trucking businesses need insurance since there are many kinds of liabilities you'll be exposed to. Insurance is often viewed as a cost by most truckers, but the fast is that it's an investment.

Tailoring a policy that fits your loads and cargo is crucial if you want to be successful in this business. Insurance is one of those things whose importance you recognize right when you need it the most.

When times are good, you'll view it as a cost. When you run into trouble and are facing a liability claim of a few hundred thousand, you'll realize how valuable it is.

Finding the perfect insurance plan for you is a tough task since there are so many liability claims you can potentially face. Educating yourself is the best place to begin.

Let's begin by examining what commercial truck insurance is and how it differs from regular auto insurance.

What Is Commercial Truck Insurance?

Commercial truck insurance is a set of policies designed to help truckers cover their needs. All of these policies cover for primary liability and then build on top of that depending on the individual trucker's needs.

Primary liability coverage is required when you're operating a truck as a bare minimum. Driving without this coverage is illegal and could result in your CDL being suspended and your vehicle impounded. This coverage protects people and property from any damage that your truck might cause.

Primary liability is often attached to a single driver. If you're operating a fleet, each of your drivers will need this coverage. If you're an owner-operator, you'll need to expand primary liability to general liability.

General liability offers additional protection for your business. While primary liability protects people and property from damage your vehicle causes, general liability protects your business from a lawsuit or libel, slander, and false advertising that might harm your business.

To operate on the road, all trucks need insurance coverage of at least $750,000. Depending on the specific type of loads you're carrying FMCSA might mandate additional insurance coverage. For example, if you're hauling cars, you'll need additional general liability coverage.

What It Covers

Commercial auto insurance is often lumped in together with commercial truck insurance but in reality, they're two different insurance coverages. Trucking is a very different activity compared to driving around town in a work van. FMCSA clearly mandates the kind of insurance policy you need if you want to operate a truck on the road.

A standard commercial auto policy will not cover your truck. In the past, many owner-operators tried to get away with this because it was cheaper, but FMCSA has cracked down on it hard.

You'll face penalties and have your CDL revoked if you try to cut costs on insurance like this. If you'll be an owner-operator, you'll have to get yourself general liability coverage. Here's what you'll be covered for:

- Bodily injury - If someone gets hurt in an accident where your truck is determined to be the primary cause of the accident, this coverage pays for medical bills and any potential lawsuits that might arise. Bodily injury also covers someone who slips and hurts themselves while on your truck. It might sound paranoid to cover yourself for this, but it never hurts to be careful.

- Damaged goods - Damaged goods covers not just someone's loads but also their property. This coverage will pay to fix and replace the property. A common occurrence in trucking is delivering goods to the wrong address or delivering wrong loads to the right address. Damaged goods or damaged commodities insurance will cover your costs for wrong deliveries. You can try to mitigate this issue as much as possible, but you'll receive addresses from carriers and freight brokers. This isn't really in your control which is why you need this coverage.

- Accidents at delivery location - Accidents might happen at your delivery location. If you or your vehicle causes any damage to property or people when delivering your goods, this coverage will cover the costs of the damage.

- Libel, slander, and false advertising - You will be advertising your brand and services to gain business. General liability coverage will protect you in case someone takes offense to your advertising and slaps you with a lawsuit claiming libel or false advertising. Many brands are hit with false advertising due to technicalities in the way they advertise themselves. Protect yourself from this by getting yourself covered under general liability.

What It Doesn't Cover

There are a few things that general liability coverage doesn't protect you from. You'll need to get yourself additional coverage for the following scenarios.

- Vehicles other than semi-trucks - This one ought to be obvious. If you're driving any vehicle other than your truck or a truck, your general liability coverage isn't going to protect you. Cement trucks, limos, hearses, buses, ice cream vans, and passenger vans are not covered by general liability.

- Driver injuries - General liability aims to protect others from your actions. It doesn't protect you from yourself. If you want to protect yourself from bodily injuries and other physical ailments, you'll need to get yourself a health insurance plan, or you'll have to opt for a worker's compensation insurance plan.

- Truck damage - Once again, general liability covers those around you from the damage you cause. It doesn't cover the costs of damages to your vehicle. To cover your truck, you'll need physical damage coverage. Technically, the law doesn't require you to obtain this coverage but it's smart business to do so.

- Damaged products due to broken cold chain technology - This is a specific scenario. If your truck's cooling breaks down and the product is damaged, general liability doesn't cover you for this. You'll have to obtain cold chain specific loss of cargo insurance. If you're planning on hauling cold chain goods, make sure you mention this to your insurance agent so that they can cover you with the right policy.

- Loss of cargo - General liability covers you for up to $5,000 worth of cargo loss but practically speaking, you'll be hauling loads worth much more than that. It's wise to get yourself expanded product coverage using one of the options I'll explain in the following sections of this chapter.

- Loss of income due to an accident - If your truck suffers damage from an accident or if you suffer an injury, it's going to take you a while to get back on the road. General liability does not cover your loss of income in this scenario. What you'll need is business interruption insurance which will cover the gaps in your income.

Other Types of Coverage

As you can see, general liability doesn't cover you for all kinds of damages out there. To fully protect yourself, you need policy add-ons that will ensure you're never without protection.

Here are additional options you should choose depending on your situation.

- Physical damage coverage - Physical damage covers all damage that occurs to your vehicle or equipment in the event of an accident. If your vehicle suffers terminal damage, the insurer will compensate you for an amount equal to the vehicle's blue book value.
- Truck cargo insurance - Also called commodity protection, this insurance coverage protects your cargo from damages that occur due to any unfortunate incidents or accidents. Often, cargo gets damaged due to being stuck in traffic jams or due to equipment failure. This coverage will ensure you're not held liable for any damages to commodities.
- Bobtail insurance - A lesser-known fact about general liability is that it only covers you when you're on a job. If you're driving around without a trailer attached, or bobtailing, traditional insurance won't cover you. Bobtail insurance covers you when you're in between jobs.

- Uninsured motorists coverage - One in eight drivers on the road today are uninsured or underinsured. If you're involved in an accident with one of these people, you could end up having to pay for damages out of pocket. Uninsured motorists coverage is an essential add-on for truckers since your replacement costs are so high.
- Reefer breakdown coverage - Cold chain trucks have a lot of sophisticated equipment on them that drivers need to worry about. If your refrigeration mechanism breaks down, you're going to be responsible for damaged products. Reefer breakdown covers the cost of lost cargo or damage to products from collisions. However, some products are excluded from this coverage. Seafood, frozen food, and tobacco are typically not covered by this. You'll need to check with your insurance agent if you're transporting these particular loads.

Costs

This is the big question. How much is all this coverage going to cost you? The short (and frustrating) answer is that it depends. Your individual situation dictates the kind of coverage you'll need to opt for. However, it's safe to say that commercial truck insurance isn't cheap. This is a direct result of the high value of goods you'll be carrying. On average, an owner-operator that opts for primary liability coverage can expect to spend around $5,000 to $7,000 per year on premiums. Again, this number varies wildly depending on the number of trucks you have or whether you have employees. Some places can run you as little as $21 per month. Here are the factors that affect the cost of insurance the most:

- Age - Your age matters. The younger you are, the greater your insurance costs will be. Of course, this doesn't mean a 99-year-old pays less than a 60-year-old. At some point, the insurance company will take your physical ability to perform the job into account.
- Driving record - Your driving record is an important factor in determining your insurance premium. If you have an accident on your record you can expect premiums to increase.
- Equipment - The age and condition of your equipment is an important part of your insurance premium. This is why I mentioned criteria in the previous chapter for used trucks. You can score great bargains on used equipment, but your insurance premiums will increase significantly.
- Loads- If you're hauling HAZMAT then your premiums will be higher compared to someone who's hauling agricultural products. Take insurance premiums into consideration before signing up to haul dangerous loads. You'll be paid more but you want to make sure your insurance isn't extremely high.
- State laws - Depending on your home state, you could end up paying higher premiums due to local laws. Florida rates are higher than anywhere else, for example (Wescott, 2019).
- Haul type - Short-hauls and local hauls generally attract lower premiums. Long-hauls have greater premiums attached to them.

Insurance costs are a significant chunk of your business and you should look to strike a balance between being covered and spending as little money as possible. Don't compromise coverage for the sake of reducing costs. However, paying top dollar for insurance isn't the smartest thing to do since those costs can add up to a significant premium over time. The best way to lower insurance costs is to have an impeccable driving record.

When operating your truck, it's best to drive safely even if it might result in a delay now and then. A great driving record reduces your premium like nothing else. Don't get a speeding ticket on your record since this will increase your premiums more than anything else except an accident in which you're liable. It's a good idea to inquire if signing up for safe driving classes with a CDL school can reduce your premiums. Typically, insurance companies are willing to do this. Inquire with your broker whether this is possible. Another option, which might be risky in some cases but is a good one nonetheless, is to raise your deductibles. A high deductible plan will lower your premium. However, the risk is that if you're in an incident you'll have to pay a high amount of money to settle the claim. Another way to reduce your premium is to pay the amount in full each year. Paying off the entire lump sum will help you capture payment discounts. If you can't afford to pay the entire premium at once, make sure you're current with your monthly payments. You don't want to be wasting your money paying late fees. Sometimes, you can reduce your premiums significantly by adjusting the type of cargo you haul, without moving out of the class entirely. For example, some insurers offer lower premiums if you carry certain "low risk" HAZMAT loads. Note that low risk here is relative. Different loads have different risk classes and every insurer treats each differently. I'll shortly cover HAZMAT insurance needs since this deserves its own section. Lastly, shop around and ask for discounts. Many owner-operators take the broker at their word and don't inquire about discounts and leave money on the table. The fact is that everything is negotiable so don't be afraid to ask for discounts.

HAZMAT Insurance

HAZMAT insurers are a class of their own since they need specialized knowledge to evaluate loads and determine premiums. Hazardous materials are regulated by stringent state and federal laws since they pose significant threats to public safety. If you're transporting these loads you need to comply with these laws and also ensure you're transporting them under the right conditions at all times. HAZMAT coverage varies but it generally falls between $1,000,000 to $5,000,000. When choosing a HAZMAT insurer, go with someone that is up to speed with DOT compliance and safety procedures. HAZMAT trucks also need additional equipment such as dashcams and other cameras that monitor the state of the load. Your insurer should know where to purchase these at the best prices possible. Here are the coverages all hazardous material transporters need:

- Pollution liability - Also called CA9948 this coverage protects you from the costs of a cleanup where pollutants were discharged onto public areas. This is a basic protection that every HAZMAT carrier ought to carry.
- Excess liability - This is an add-on to primary liability and covers the trucker for up to $50,000,000. This coverage is

needed when transporting petroleum and other valuable goods whose cargo value is extremely high.

- Collision and comprehensive - This protects not just your truck but also the trailer in case of collision, fire, theft, and any other adverse event.

- HAZMAT general liability- This is different from general liability that you'll carry automatically as an owner-operator. HAZMAT general liability protects you from wrong deliveries and damages that arise from it.

- Combined deductibles - In case of damage to your physical self and cargo, you can pay just one deductible to account for both coverages.

- Loading and unloading - This covers you against damages that might occur when cargo is being loaded or unloaded.

- Medical and personal injury - This coverage pays medical expenses to you and any passengers in your truck if they're injured in an accident, irrespective of who is at fault.

- Downtime - If you have an incident that results in either an injury to you or leaves your truck inoperable, you should opt for downtime coverage. This will help you cover your bills while you recover. While different insurers provide different coverages, most of them offer cash payment of around $150 per day for 60 days. A lot depends on your particular policy so make sure to check these terms with your insurer.

- Lease or loan gap - A common occurrence that owner-operators have to watch out for is becoming upside down on their vehicle financing. This occurs when the vehicle or trailer depreciates quickly and leaves you owing more on the financing than what the vehicle is worth. For example, if you lease a three-year-old $60,000 used truck, the vehicle has already experienced most of its depreciation. You're unlikely to end up in a scenario where you owe $50,000 on the lease but your truck is worth just $40,000. With new trucks, there is a danger of this happening since depreciation is at its steepest in the first two years. Loan or lease gap coverage protects you from this happening.

- Rental reimbursement - If your truck is inoperable following an accident, you can rent a truck to carry out your business. Of course, this rented truck comes with its own costs and many operators find them massive. Rental reimbursement coverage pays a significant chunk of rental costs so you can continue with business as usual while your primary vehicle gets repaired.

As I mentioned previously, HAZMAT insurance is its own world and you should not choose insurance coverage based on the price you're quoted. Always take the time to shop around but match appropriate coverage to the costs you'll have to pay. Don't opt for the cheapest insurance but don't automatically assume that the most expensive insurance is the best. Understand the different coverages you need to opt for. For example, if you choose to haul radioactive waste, your insurance requirements are going to be very different from that of an oil and gas hauler. It's impossible to go into the details of each and every hazardous product out there so make sure you speak to a reliable HAZMAT insurance provider and understand your options.

Applying for Insurance

The truck insurance application process is straightforward but there are a few potholes you need to avoid. The steps I'll outline next will save you a lot of time and will help you avoid these costly mistakes.

Contact

The first step is to contact a reliable motor carrier insurance agent. If you're searching online type those exact words into the search bar. Searching for "truck insurance" or "truckers insurance" might not give you the right results.

Understand that trucking insurance isn't cheap. All insurance agents will need some basic information before they provide you with a quote. This information includes:

- Type of vehicle and number of them if you're operating a fleet
- Load type - Describe this in as much detail as possible
- Haul times and location - will you be short-hauling, long-hauling or running locally?

How can you evaluate an insurance provider? The easiest way to determine good providers is to speak to other truckers and get recommendations. Make sure you're talking to owner-operators since company drivers don't have to worry too much about insuring their vehicles or cargo. If you can't contact independent owner-operators for some reason, search online or on forums. Facebook groups are a great place to source recommendations. You will receive offers from agents lurking on those groups but make sure you carry out your research thoroughly.

The first step is to evaluate the extent of their network. A national network is preferable. However, if you're concentrating on hauling loads within a certain region or area, you can opt for agents who have a strong presence in these locations. The presence of a network doesn't mean you'll get great service automatically.

It's just that a national provider will be more entrenched in the locations they're present in. If you have a breakdown in Georgia, calling your agent representative office in Texas isn't going to ensure the timely arrival of a mechanic. However, the presence of a local office will ensure that the staff there have better local knowledge and can service you potentially faster. Customer service is perhaps the biggest indicator of an insurance provider's reliability. You can glean many clues during the signup process. Notice how willing the agent is to answer your questions and how well they explain everything to you. An agent that is incentivized to simply bring as many clients into the shop is working for a bad company. A good insurance provider is your partner in business. They're the ones protecting you from liability or worse, so make sure you choose them wisely. Check online for reviews of their service and what people are saying about them. Pay attention to negative reviews since these offer insight into how bad situations are handled. The mere presence of a negative review isn't a red flag. Make sure you read them in detail and evaluate the provider in a balanced manner.

Determine Coverage

Once you've chosen the right insurance provider you need to figure out what coverage you'll need. FMCSA specifies the following coverage as the bare minimum (*Step by Step Guide to Getting Your Trucking Insurance*, 2020):

- Public liability - This covers bodily injury, property damage, and any environmental damage you might have caused
- Freight up to $5,000,000 with a minimum of $75,000 depending on the cargo.
- Non-HAZMAT loads under 10,000 lbs must be insured for up to $300,000.
- Household goods carriers have additional coverage they must obtain:
  - Cargo insurance of $5,000 per vehicle
  - Cargo insurance must also cover $10,000 worth of damage per incident.
- HAZMAT carriers must be insured for a minimum of $1,000,000 up to $5,000,000 depending on the load.

The optional coverages you can opt for have already been described in this chapter previously. It's best to stay as safe as possible of course but this doesn't mean you should automatically opt for every coverage out there. Speak to your agent in detail and have them explain each coverage and the fine print that goes along with it. It's also a good idea to speak to experienced truckers to figure out what you need.

You'll often hear truckers say that they "don't need" this kind of coverage or that kind. While practical input is great, you have no assurance that these old truckers are up to speed with legal requirements. It's best to play it safe when starting out and listen to what your insurance agent recommends.

Fill Out the Forms

Your agent will supply you with all the forms you need to fill out to obtain insurance. These forms are quite straightforward to fill out. Make sure you use the proper business name throughout all of them. For example, if you've applied for your FMCSA authority as "J Smith Trucking LLC" don't fill out your insurance form as "John Smith Trucking". Those are two different entities entirely. As I mentioned previously, even a misplaced period in your business name is considered a different entity by the authorities. You'll need to provide your EIN numbers when applying for insurance so make sure you have this ready. As proof, your agent will ask you to furnish them with copies of your company license and formation agreements. If you're operating as an LLC, you can provide them with the articles and the initial filing that you filed with the state registrar. Once you've filled out your forms, all you need to do is wait.

Follow Up

Once your forms are properly filled out, your agent will send them to FMCSA for approval. This is an important step in the process and without it, you will not receive your authority. To be able to conduct business with your MC number, FMCSA needs to have received your insurance forms. You'll need to send these forms to the authorities within 90 days of receiving your MC number and applying for your authority. Most insurance agents are great at sending your paperwork over and it's unlikely you'll have issues. However, in the off chance that an issue does occur, you should follow up with them and ask them for a receipt that proves they've forwarded your paperwork to FMCSA. In terms of timing, you can schedule to apply for your insurance and other paperwork during the 10-day protest period once you receive your MC number. As I mentioned earlier, you'll also need your process agent to send the BOC-3 form to FMCSA. Unlike the BOC-3 form, you cannot send your insurance forms in yourself. FMCSA mandates that the insurance agent be the one to send in all relevant paperwork.

Insurance Renewal

Most owner-operators leave the insurance process as is once they receive their authority and neglect to think of it ever again. The typical policy lasts for three years, with some even lasting as long as five years or as little as one. When the time comes for renewal, they're in for a rude shock since they automatically assume that their rates will remain the same. Unfortunately, it's extremely rare that insurance rates will remain stable. In most cases, the average cost of insurance per mile will increase. It's estimated that the cost of insurance per mile increases by two cents every year. This situation is extremely frustrating for truckers and owner-operators, but there isn't much they can do about it. Neither can your insurance agent help you out with this. It's just the nature of the business. Rates are usually set by companies and by faceless machines that have no idea how good a driver you are. If a company has a large number of claims issued against them, they'll automatically increase premiums on existing policies to recoup some of that money. Of course, your own rate of filing claims counts against you. File even a single claim and your premium is sure to rise. Your driving record is also important in determining what you'll pay upon renewal. Keep your record as clean as possible.

While you might be partial towards choosing luxury equipment with the fanciest features, these come at a cost. Thanks to the value of your equipment being greater, your insurance premium will also be greater. If you expand your fleet from a single truck to multiple ones, your insurance quote will increase on a per truck basis.

As your policy comes to a close, you will begin to receive calls from insurance agents. This is because insurance information is public, and you can expect calls to start flooding within 90 days of expiry. Again, it's best to evaluate all the offers you receive on the basis of the coverage you're opting for, not just the prices you're being quoted. Don't automatically assume your existing agent cannot match a lower price. While they might not be able to offer you a price that is lower than your current premium, they will have room to provide you a premium that is lower than what another agent is offering. A good insurance agent will start sending feelers for renewal 90 days out from policy expiration. While you should conduct your own research, it's best to stick to your existing agent if everything has been going well with them. There's no need to fix something that isn't broken after all.

If your current agent isn't checking up on you to inquire about renewal or behaves as if your business isn't valuable to them, you should switch agents. Again, evaluate everything from the perspective of coverage, not just cost. There are some occasions where you might receive a notice of non-renewal. This notice is usually sent 30-60 days before expiry. A non-renewal notice comes in two flavors. The first situation is a negative one where your claims are increasing in severity or where your risk profile has moved into unacceptable territory for the insurer. If you've had multiple serious violations or accidents, you can expect this notice to arrive. Receiving a few tickets isn't a serious enough violation so don't worry about those scenarios. Your existing insurer will note that they're opting to not renew your coverage due to your safety record and this impacts your ability to find new coverage. You'll need to shop heavily and widely to get covered once again and will have to pay high premiums. One option is to choose short term policies that can re-establish the fact that you are a responsible and safe driver.

The second scenario is a neutral one that doesn't affect your ability to procure new insurance. If your insurer moves out of the business of insuring truckers or doesn't wish to provide insurance to truckers who carry the type of loads you do, you'll receive a notice of non-renewal. This isn't a serious situation and you can easily find a new insurer to replace them. A non-renewal notice is extremely negative mostly to truckers who are carrier-financed. I've already explained why this is a poor option. However, if you find yourself in this position, understand that insurance is usually handled by your carrier directly. If your carrier opts out of the business, then you're in a sticky situation. You'll likely have to find a new carrier and truck since your original carrier won't let you carry your truck over to a new carrier. All in all, it's best to avoid falling into the carrier financing trap altogether. This brings to a close our look at trucking insurance options for owner-operators. As you can see, there's a lot to digest and with good reason. Your insurance policy is your primary protection against disasters of any kind. Unfortunately, many truckers look at insurance as an added cost. This is the wrong view to adopt since it could lead you to choosing a less-than-ideal policy for your business. Take the time to talk to other truckers and also insurance agents. Some truckers erroneously assume that every insurance agent is out to get them, but this isn't the case. An insurance agent is simply doing their job so don't assume they're out to rob you. A good insurance agent is your partner in business and if they do their job well, they'll keep you out of the courts and far away from bankruptcy. Make sure you shop around before settling on a policy. There are different coverages you'll need to choose to properly protect yourself. Depending on your loads, you'll have to opt for different coverages. So, make sure you conduct your research thoroughly before signing up for a policy. Review the information in this chapter before shopping for insurance. This will allow you to ask the right questions when you speak to an agent.

Chapter 6:
Running Your Business

Getting your licenses in order and buying the right equipment is great, but it won't count for much unless you can back it up with efficient office processes. Unfortunately, this is the portion of their business that most truckers ignore. The fact is that getting the right official documents and whatnot is just the start. You need to execute a bunch of other processes to run your business efficiently. As a trucker, you won't be in a physical office, but this doesn't mean you shouldn't have a business location.

Many owner-operators list their home address as their office address. This is fine but it helps to set aside space in your home where you can store your business assets. You'll need a computer, a desk, and a phone at the very least. Besides, setting aside separate space in your home helps you with tax reporting as well.

The IRS allows you to deduct office expenditures from your revenues, but you need to prove to them that you've dedicated space to running your business. Another option is to band together with other truckers and lease office space.

Splitting the costs will help you gain an office space as well as help you reduce the financial burden on yourself. Once you've decided on a space, the next step is to furnish it. This isn't particularly difficult. You'll need a desk and a chair at the very least. If you're planning on starting a fleet right off the bat, I'll address these needs shortly. For now, as an owner-operator, all you need is a desk and chair, along with some filing cabinets to store relevant papers.

You will need a computer and software to handle business needs. I'll discuss these later in this chapter. For now, let's move on and take a look at what you'll need in your office if you're looking at starting a fleet right now. Even if you're an owner-operator, it will be of immense value for you to read this section since many requirements apply to you as well.

Office Requirements for Fleet Operators

The word fleet conjures images of thousands of trucks but if technically speaking, if you're running two trucks, you're still a fleet operator. It's a step up from being an owner-operator.

At some point, as your fleet grows, you'll be better served sitting in your office as opposed to driving your truck. The first task is to find good office space.

You don't need anything lavish, nor do you need an office that is in a high-end part of town. All you need is space that you can use to conduct business. After all, your clients are not going to evaluate you based on where your office is.

Employees

To succeed in fleet management, you need to hire good employees. If you're managing under five trucks, you'll be fine with a single employee, assuming you're driving one of the trucks. This person will be in charge of operations and daily office tasks. This person should ideally be well organized and should have the ability to communicate well. Since you'll be on the road for the most part, they should be comfortable talking on the phone. Email or text communications won't cut it. It also helps to hire another person who can carry out marketing and sales tasks for you.

Some fleet owners view this as an unnecessary cost. In all fairness, hiring a salesperson might be overkill but it depends on the depth of contacts you have in the industry. If you have deep contacts and a full pipeline, you don't need a sales team (or person.) However, if you're uncertain of how stacked your pipeline is, you should design sales processes and have a person execute them.

The most critical part of your operation is the finances. You need someone who can keep track of your invoices. Most truckers get paid on a 60-90 days credit cycle. This makes tracking invoices challenging. If your operation is small, you can have the same person who manages your office track invoices.

Once your business expands, you'll need to have a person carry out this task. This person will need to call your customers, track invoices, and deposit cash in your business' bank account. Financial tracking doesn't stop there. You'll need the services of an accountant to keep track of your financial statements and tax reporting. When your company is small, think under 10 trucks operational, you can outsource these tasks to a qualified accountant. Do not choose the cheapest service provider. A good accountant will literally help you find money through tax credits and other deductions that will help you hang onto more of your cash.

Many owner-operators treat accounting services as an expense, and this is a mistake. Outsourcing it to your cousin just because they took a few courses isn't the way to go about this. Talk to other business owners (not just truckers) to get recommendations of good accountants. Make sure you ask them questions about their experience in the business. Handling depreciation is one of the biggest concerns you'll have as a business owner so focus on this topic. Ask them how they'll handle it and whether you could run into any issues if it's handled too aggressively. You'll have to use software to help you manage loads so it's a good idea to have someone on call who can sort out any IT issues. You don't want your business to come to a halt because your computer won't start.

Office Equipment

You'll need a computer at the very least. It doesn't have to be an extremely powerful machine. Anything with an Intel i5 and above or equivalent will suit you well. You will need a scanner and printer access. You can opt for a printer plus scanner machine that will do the job for you. There are many such machines you can buy on the market for a cheap price. Shop online for them and get the lowest price possible.

When it comes to printers, opt for one that uses the least amount of ink. Replacing ink cartridges is a hidden cost of printing. Don't be misled by a cheap price. Cartridge costs can add up over the course of the lifetime of the printer and burn a hole in your pocket. Realistically speaking, that is all a small fleet operation needs. As your business grows, you'll need to move into larger office space and they'll need computers, office furniture, and other infrastructure to support their job functions. Start off small and scale gradually.

Software

This is perhaps the most important part of your infrastructure. These days you cannot conduct business successfully without the right software. Older truckers can get by with their deep contacts and some of them might even be hostile to software. However, don't expect to succeed if you cannot use software the right way. As a trucker, you'll have to install an electronic logging device or ELD software at the very least. This software is a Federally mandated requirement so it's not as if you can avoid this. I'll explain this software's objective in the next chapter, along with the legalities it covers. ELD software is usually an app that you can install on your smartphone (and on that of your drivers) to track relevant data.

It syncs with a desktop app that allows you to quickly view relevant data and plan your fleet better. The second piece of software you need is a Transportation Management Software or TMS. This is an all in one software that handles all of your day-to-day business needs as well as compliance requirements. Trucking is a compliance heavy business and you need software that will help you remain up to date with regard to all of the paperwork you'll need to file. One of the primary compliance requirements is IFTA reporting. As I mentioned earlier, IFTA is a new fuel tax system that applies to North America. You'll need to calculate your mileage in every state your trucks operate in and report relevant taxes to each state separately.

Calculating mileage and then appropriate fuel tax is a huge headache as you can imagine. Instead, the best way to handle it is to use software that does it for you. If you're a one-person owner-operator or even someone who runs a fleet of 50 trucks, you need to keep track of your dispatches. Your dispatch log is a list of who needs what loads moved to which destination.

If you're a solitary operator, this particular feature might not be of the greatest use to you since you can track everything yourself. However, if you're operating a fleet of even two trucks, it comes in handy. There are many issues that crop up when managing a fleet and almost all of them are addressed by cash. For example, if the other driver in your fleet suffers a mechanical breakdown and needs to fix it, they need cash. It'll be impossible for you to send them cash on the spot, so they'll have to spend it out of pocket before you reimburse them.

This doesn't sound like a huge issue but tracking cash spends and advances like this is an accounting nightmare. A good dispatch software helps you tally cash balances that you can feed into your accounting software. Once your business grows, staying in touch with customers becomes difficult. You need to remember their names, phone numbers, and emails. A good CRM or customer relationship management software is essential and every TMS comes with an inbuilt package to achieve this. You can edit customer information, send automated emails from your business email account, and even set up specific event reminders that will help you stay in touch with them. This way you can ensure that you always remain near the top of their mind. TMS software also has a powerful analytics package that allows you to review your fuel usage, load expenses, and other costs that hurt your bottom line. You'll be able to map your routes more efficiently and save more money.

Think of it as an investment, not a cost. Issuing invoices is also easy with a TMS since you'll be able to seamlessly link your customer information with load information to generate a payment request. Automating invoice issuance is a key process if you want to stay on top of your business. The third piece of software you'll need to install is bookkeeping software such as Quickbooks or Zoho Books.

This software will help you stay on top of expenses as you go about your business. In fact, you'll be able to provide your accountant a link to your software and they'll be able to prepare financial statements using information there. Bookkeeping isn't accounting. Instead, it's a process of recording all expenses into ledgers that apply to different portions of your financial statements.

The process of determining which expense goes into which ledger and how those amounts translate to a financial statement is a tedious one. Software will help you take care of all of this and will automate the process for you. Even if you're an owner-operator, you'll need an ELD and bookkeeping software at the very least. There are many options you can choose from within these categories. Here are a few top picks. Make sure to carry out your own research since your needs might be different. ELD Software - This software comes with devices that plug into your truck in different ways. The data they collect is transmitted to an app on your phone and desktop.

- KeepTruckin - This is the cheapest ELD software out there. It costs $20 per month and offers a free trial. It's a good, all-round ELD that might not be as sophisticated as some of the other choices on this list, but if you're budget-conscious, this is the best way to go. Note that the basic plan doesn't include IFTA fuel tracking. For that feature, you'll need to pay an additional $10 per month. In fact, many add ons require additional charges. Realistically speaking you'll need to pay around $50 to access all of its features to run a business.

- Garmin eLog - The eLog is slightly different from the rest of the software on this list. It's old school in that you pay just once for lifetime use. The cost is $250 which sounds like a lot but given its long life, it's a great investment. The con is that there's a steep learning curve you'll have to master. There is a very strong customer support team and you can easily track fuel usage that you can integrate with a TMS. This means all of your software can talk to each other and you don't have to manage everything manually.

- Samsara ELD - Samsara is the option that has the most features and is also the most expensive. You'll pay $99 initially for the device followed by $30 per month to access the software. There is a free trial version you can take out for a spin before paying. The learning curve on this app is easy and it plugs into almost everything which makes using it really simple. Add to this the almost constant free upgrades and you'll always have an app that's ready to go. Samsara also offers TMS solutions so integrating it with their suite is easy. However, the app also integrates with other TMS platforms.

- GPS Trackit ELD - At $24.95 per month, this option lands somewhere in between the other choices. In terms of software, there's nothing truly remarkable that sets it apart from the previous options. However, the key selling point that this software has is that there are no contracts. You can stop at any time and suspend your billing. With the other options, you'll be locked into a one-year contract. In Garmin's case, it's for life since you'll pay an upfront cost. No commitment is the mantra here. You don't have to opt for their device and can plug their software into the hardware of your choice. The features are limited but it features a robust suite of customizable alerts that can be tailored for almost every need.

The second software pillar your business needs is TMS. There are many options on the market but here are some of the best ones you can choose.

- 3Gtms - This is probably the best option for small fleet owners. The software is endlessly customizable and is tailored for the North American market. While the larger features might be inapplicable for your small business, even the pared-down version will be of use to a small fleet operator. If you're an owner-operator, you probably don't need this software.
- Ascend TMS - Ascend is one of the most popular names in the business and is used by almost everyone in the industry.
- Cloud Logistics - This is an up and coming company in the shipping industry and is focused on trucking.

The costs of these software programs varies depending on your needs. For example, 3Gtms can cost as much as $10,000 upfront. Does this mean you need it? Not quite. Your needs are specific to you and it helps to speak to the software sales team to evaluate whether this is for you. If you're running an owner-operator business, you probably don't need a TMS. Accounting software is an integral part of your business. While most accounting software will do the trick for you, you'll need to customize them to fit the needs of your trucking business. It's better to opt for solutions that have been designed with truckers in mind.

- Quickbooks online - This is the most popular and comprehensive option. While it isn't designed just for truckers, it fits the needs of most small businesses. As a result, you're guaranteed support at all times. You can even sync the desktop software with a mobile app to enter expenses on the go. Quickbooks integrates with ELD software and this helps you track mileage for IFTA purposes. There is a wide range of pricing tiers, so you'll need to explore the app to fully understand what you need. You will need additional customization to make it work for your trucking business.

- Q7 - Q7 is best suited for medium to large-sized trucking companies and fleet managers. However, it is well suited for owner-operators as well, even if some of its features might be overkill. All of your trucking business' needs are built into the app and you don't need to customize anything. The downside is that there is no free trial and you'll need to contact the company directly for pricing. If you happen to use a Mac, Q7 will not work for you since it's incompatible.

- Axon - If you plan on scaling your business quickly, then Axon is a good choice for you. It's targeted specifically towards mid-sized trucking companies and integrates with different trucking software on every truck in your fleet. Like Q7, you need to contact the vendor to obtain pricing and installation can be a bit of a drag with on-site installation needed. However, financial reporting is excellent. You will still need the services of a CPA to help you figure out your taxes.

- TruckingOffice - This app is built specifically for owner-operators, but it lacks some functionality that can help you automate invoicing and payment follow-ups. If you're unwilling to hire someone to manage this for you, executing these tasks manually can become tedious. However, when it comes to IFTA fuel reporting, there's no contest between this and the other apps. When combined with its ability to integrate with other trucking apps, and the fact that it's designed for small trucking operations, the pros outweigh the cons.

Make sure you research all of the options above before choosing one. Your business' needs are unique, and you should carefully consider all features before settling on a choice.

What You Should Do and What to Outsource

As you can see there are many tasks that go along with running a business successfully. The question that most trucking operators have is which tasks ought to be outsourced and which ones need to be executed by the owners themselves. A lot of this is self-explanatory but for the sake of clarity, let's just say that all trucking-related tasks such as finding loads, marketing, and dispatching should be executed by you. Back-office duties such as bookkeeping, administrative tasks, and expense recording should be outsourced either to an employee or to an accountant. I'll address compliance reporting in detail in the next chapter. Compliance reports will be a collaborative effort between you and an employee. You'll need to enter the relevant data into an app or in your notes and your employee can consolidate the numbers before reporting it to the relevant authorities. It's helpful to execute your tasks step by step before deciding on a final framework. Execute the tasks that you enjoy working on and outsource the rest to other people.

Organizing Your Finances

One of the things that routinely trips up owner-operators is their finances. To be precise, it's the lack of organization in their finances that trips them up. A trucking business is all about managing cash flow and finding loads. You can find all the loads you want but if you don't manage and project your cash flow accurately, you're going to find yourself with an empty bank account and a stack of unpaid invoices. Before I list tips to help you organize your cash flow, it's important to note that the logistics industry works on credit cycles. This is because everyone pays everyone else well after loads have been moved. Therefore, if you happen to encounter a broker or a shipper that specifies a 60-day credit cycle, don't take this as an instance of them trying to put one over you.

They themselves probably get paid after this period and don't have cash to pay you once you deliver the load. The other issue is that problems often occur with loads. From a trucker's perspective, the delivery address or the load quantity might be incorrect. You'll still get paid for delivering these loads but from your customer's perspective, it's understandable that they won't be willing to immediately release payment for erroneous loads. In such cases, insurance companies get involved and your customer will wait for insurance payouts before settling payment.

This is why it's helpful to always work with a reliable broker or customer. The more errors they make, the more your payment gets delayed. If you decide to operate HAZMAT loads, you'll have to wait for at least 60 days before getting paid.

This is because these loads require a lot of compliance checks that customers have to carry out before releasing payment. They will need to verify your logs and the conditions under which the goods were transported. Therefore, despite the higher payouts, the length of the credit cycle and insurance can dampen your margins.

Despite all of this, managing your cash flow is as simple as following a few tried and tested best practices. Let's look at some of them now.

Always Follow Up

Many truckers think that getting paid is as simple as issuing an invoice and then waiting for cash to arrive. This isn't true at all. In fact, you'll have to follow up at least twice before getting paid. I'm not trying to say that your customers will swindle you out of your cash. It's just that everyone gets paid late so make following up a routine part of your process. It's best to create a time-based process for this. If your invoices are automated, it saves you time. You can also program automated follow-ups into your software. If you have an employee, you can have them follow up with customers at intervals of 15 days, 30 days, 45 days, and 60 days. Typically, you can expect payment within a 60-day cycle. However, you will run into the occasional 90-day cycle which can be tough to deal with.

I'll shortly explain how you can avoid this nightmare. For now, just understand that following up is a routine part of your business.

You can either automate it or outsource it. Above all else, remember that your customers are also being paid on a delayed cycle so there isn't much point in you complaining to them about being paid late.

Focus on Quality

A common mistake beginner owner-operators make is to take every job that's out there. Often, jobs that come easily to you do so for a reason. It's because every other experienced trucker knows to stay far away from it. It doesn't matter what niche you're in, there are always a few bad apples that sour the bunch. Focus on working with high-quality customers and shippers and you won't have as many cash flow problems. Bad quality customers routinely make mistakes in the bills of lading (BoL) and rarely pay you within a reasonable time period. In fact, a bad customer will pay you somewhere in the 90-day region, because that's all they can afford. A good customer will ensure you get paid within 60 days or so even if they haven't been paid. These people can afford to pay you in this time because they have access to financing that helps them tide over any cash-flow gap. Financing plays a major role in helping logistics companies overcome cash flow problems but to access it one needs to have great credit. A bank or an invoice factoring company (a company that loans money against outstanding invoices) isn't going to simply give its money away to anyone that knocks on their door. To receive financing, companies need to have a solid client list, a good reputation, and stellar credit. A bad company has none of these things and this is why they'll delay paying you out. One of the things to look for when signing up for loads is to see how long the post or requirement has been active. For example, a load that has been active for over a week on a load board (I'll explain these shortly) but hasn't been picked up as yet is a red flag. Either the load itself is too niched (for example HAZMAT) or the shipper is troublesome to deal with. If the load is extremely specialized, then a week-long waiting period isn't a red flag by itself. It's best to network with other truckers and get the scoop on some of the shippers who advertise on load boards.

Use Load Boards Wisely

A load board is an online load listing community that aims to connect truckers with shippers. For example, if a manufacturer of furniture needs goods shipped from Texas to Nebraska, a load board is where they'll go. Mind you, a load board isn't their first choice. Every shipper or manufacturer works with their own carrier or a freight broker. These intermediaries farm work out to truckers and this is how the best loads are found. The ones that make it to load boards either contain terms that aren't acceptable for most truckers or have some kind of stipulation that makes it impossible for a broker to work with it. Not every load on a load board is tainted. Often, shippers choose load boards because they get to work with truckers directly. This is often the case with smaller companies that wish to remove intermediaries from the chain and lower their shipping costs. Here are some good load boards you can sign up for:

- Trucker Path
- truckstop.com
- Direct Freight
- 123loadboard
- DAT load board

Load boards are great when you're starting out but don't make it a habit to rely on them exclusively. This is because it's hard to form a strong relationship with your shipper when you source work from a load board. Like with job vacancies, the best loads aren't advertised. You'll be able to access these loads only if you forge strong customer relationships. I'll explain how you can carry out effective marketing that ensures this later in this book. For now, feel free to use load boards to get started and to help you tide over and short-term cash flow problems. Remember that you'll get paid 60 days down the road so it might take you some time to see a return on your investment. However, load boards are a great option for you to choose when starting out since you'll be able to pick up some work quickly.

Keep a Cash Reserve

This tip applies to every business out there but is uniquely suited for truckers thanks to the economics of being an owner-operator. Always have a reserve amount of cash in your bank account and don't rely on customer payments to pay for emergency expenses. There will always be unexpected expenses that crop up and you'll need to take care of them with cash.

For example, you could be on a long haul and your equipment suffers damage. In such situations, you'll need a reserve of cash to not just pay for expenses but to also tide you over the period where you'll lose income from having to wait for repairs. Even if you're covered for downtime through your insurance policy, it takes time for claims to settle and for payouts to begin. Don't rely on customers to bail you out either. For example, if you know that you have a major expense coming up in 60 days and are expecting a customer to clear an invoice and use that cash, you're running your business incorrectly. While it's great to have customer cash flow routinely, you shouldn't put yourself in a position to expect it to bail you out of trouble. Always plan to have a reserve of at least four months' expenses in your bank account. The problem with estimating this amount is that expenses vary. After all, some costs are front-loaded while others are monthly. To solve this issue, calculate your annual expenses and divide that number by 12 to get your true monthly expense. Now multiply this number by four and that's how much you need to have in the bank at a minimum. Your cash reserve should be placed in a bank account that is separate from your personal account. Many truckers make the mistake of combining their personal finances with their business finances and I've already explained why this is a big mistake. You lose limited liability protection (potentially) if you don't separate your finances. Keep your business cash separate and you'll be fine.

Track Everything

Good financial management is about discipline more than anything else. It's easy to fall into poor habits and forget to jot down expenses when you incur them. Make it a point to save all of your receipts and to record them into your bookkeeping app. There's no shortcut to this process, you'll have to do the work yourself.

If your app has a mobile version your task is a bit easier since you can enter it directly into the software. However, you still need to save your receipts. This can get cumbersome and it might seem pointless. However, the IRS can decide to audit your tax returns and will ask for receipts as proof of expenses. It's better to be prepared and save everything rather than run the risk of paying a penalty.

You should also store all of your invoices and other important documents either in digital or paper format. These days, most TMSs allow you to invoice clients so you don't need to print paper. If you're not using a TMS, make sure you save the electronic copy of the invoice on your office computer before sending it out. Once it's paid, make sure you record this as well. It'll make following up on invoices a lot easier.

If you're not going to be hiring an employee to manage reconciling payments to invoices, make sure you set aside a week every month to carry out this process. It's a critical function in your business, and the last thing you want is for your customers to tell you they've already paid you, but you can't find the check they mailed. Digitizing this process is the best solution. Send invoices electronically and give your customers the ability to pay you electronically as well instead of mailing you a check. You'll have to set aside time to collect the check and manually deposit it. You'll then need to wait another couple of days for the check to clear. Skip this hassle by allowing them to pay you by credit card or through an eCheck. You can ask your CPA for recommendations for software that will allow you to do this seamlessly. Alternatively, you can use Quickbooks or any accounting software to issue invoices and collect payments.

Budget for Maintenance

Maintaining your equipment is a crucial part of your business and you must always set aside cash to pay for this. Many truckers ignore this and only address issues when they get out of hand. Aside from the safety aspect of maintaining your truck, the biggest issue with ignoring routine maintenance is that it becomes expensive to operate your truck in the long run.

There's no set amount I can give you for this expense since so much depends on the kind of equipment you're running. It's best to speak to your dealer and mechanics to figure out what you can expect to pay for maintenance.

Routine maintenance will have to be carried out at periodic intervals so calculate the total for a year and divide that number by 12 to arrive at the monthly expense.

Ask for Help

A common mistake that most business owners make is to think they need to do everything themselves. This is a normal tendency since many business owners tend to be driven people who are used to getting things done and getting results. However, you cannot hope to make your business successful if you plan on doing everything by yourself. After all, you can't drive your truck and calculate your taxes at the same time! Some owner-operators are loath to hire out tasks because they look at it as an expense. While other people's expertise costs money, look at this as the cost of getting your time back for yourself. You can use this time to do the things that are important to you. For example, would you rather spend time with your family, or would you rather spend that time calculating taxes and filing regulatory paperwork? Ask experienced truckers for help and network with them. You'll find them more than happy to help you out. Seek the help of professionals in areas that you aren't an expert in.

Pay them for their time and you'll find it much easier to run your business.

Remain Compliant

Compliance is your biggest headache as an owner-operator. There are a number of things you should be aware of when running a trucking business and violating any of these regulations will result in a hefty penalty. It can seem intimidating to track every single regulation out there which is why I've gathered all of this information into a single chapter. While the next chapter will give you all the information you need to remain compliant, making sure you actually are compliant is all about executing simple processes.

Keep meticulous records and don't neglect to keep copies of receipts and bills. To comply with some regulations, you'll need to use software so don't try to compromise on those costs. Let's now take a look at the regulations that all truck operators have to remain aware of and comply with.

Zachary Bosch

Chapter 7: Compliance

Driving a truck is a tough task. Not only are you in control of a huge vehicle that is carrying precious cargo, a small misstep by you on the highways can put other people in danger. To mitigate this, the government has designed a number of regulations that keep our roads safe and you along with it. There's also the issue of being environmentally friendly. Trucks have huge engines that (mostly) run on diesel. This has an impact on the environment and with sustainability issues becoming more important than ever before, many states have enacted laws that restrict the use and operation of trucks. Operating from another state and merely transiting through another state isn't a valid excuse for being non-compliant with the transit state's environmental laws. Lastly, there are compliance requirements with respect to your licensing and other paperwork from FMCSA. These are pretty straightforward and are rarely a hassle. However, you should be aware of them nonetheless. All of the regulations described in this chapter can be found at https://www.ecfr.gov/cgi-bin/text-idx?SID=0b8823936fb0bcb20b7ae23a9d50e909&c=ecfr&tpl=/ecfr browse/Title49/49cfrv5_02.tpl#300

which is the government's repository for all rules pertaining to motor vehicle carriers. Let's begin by addressing federal compliance rules.

FMCSA Rules

FMCSA is the federal body you'll be reporting to and their laws form the bulk of regulations you'll have to comply with. If you're an owner-operator or a fleet manager, you'll need to be aware of these laws. Note that FMCSA changes its laws from time to time so you should always check to see if your compliance status is up to date. While there are many regulations to be aware of, the most important sections deal with Hours of Service (HOS), Driver Vehicle Inspection Reports (DVIRs), drug testing, and Compliance and Safety Standards or CSA. CSA is vast enough to warrant its own section and I'll get to it shortly. FMCSA does a pretty thorough job of taking every party's needs into account before coming up with laws. The body conducts annual surveys of crash and accident data and devises rules that are geared towards increasing road safety. They also conduct hearings and commission studies to determine the efficacy of their rules.

Here are the primary concerns that all FMCSA regulation aims to address (*Hours of Service*, 2013):

- Driver safety - The driver in question is both you as well as other people driving their vehicles on the road
- Trucker qualification - Driving a big rig isn't an easy job. It's in everyone's best interests that all drivers be qualified to carry out this task.
- Drug testing - Drug and alcohol testing is a major part of keeping the roads safe.
- Vehicle safety - Even the best drivers cannot overcome a compromised rig. Vehicle inspections and safety are of paramount concern.
- Cargo security- This applies to HAZMAT loads that require special compliance

Let's begin by looking at the HOS rules in detail.

HOS or Hours of Service

If you possess a CDL in the United States, you're subject to HOS rules. HOS is a perennial topic of contention between truckers and FMCSA. While both parties aim to ensure maximum safety, there are times when the rules can get excessive. HOS rules outline how long a driver can operate their truck before they are required to take breaks. A fatigued driver is a hazard to everyone on the road and this is what HOS aims to prevent. Despite the seemingly simple goal, these rules can get a bit complicated. HOS rules were first published in 2011 and have been modified heavily since then. Back when they were first published, drivers were required to maintain driving logs on paper. These days, paper is unacceptable, and every truck must be outfitted with an electronic logging device or ELD. An ELD plus directly into your truck's engine and logs the time it spends in action, idling, etc.

ELDs also capture other important vehicle data so don't think they're useful just for compliance purposes. They can help you save fuel and analyze your idling patterns. This can help you reduce running costs. Returning to compliance, your ELD will be examined by inspectors to ensure you're staying on the right side of HOS regulations.

There are four statuses that ELDs primarily record. The first is the off-duty status that is self-explanatory. It switches on when your truck isn't running. The sleeper berth status indicates you're resting in the cab's sleeping area and is also an inactive status.

The Driving status indicates the truck is in operation and finally, the On Duty status indicates times when the truck isn't moving, but the driver is either idling or is carrying out some task that is related to moving their loads. As a trucker, your life will revolve around these four statuses quite a bit.

This is because all HOS rules center around how long you can spend in one of these statuses. A driver can operate their vehicle for up to 11 hours before taking a mandatory 10-hour break. Note that these 11 hours refer to the Driving status and don't include On Duty time. The maximum time window a driver can spend On Duty is 14 hours.

Logically speaking, this means you can drive for 11 hours within a 14-hour window, with the remaining three hours spent either taking a short break or carrying out vehicle inspection tasks. At the end of your 14-hour window or the 11-hour Driving window, you must take a 10-

hour break at the very least. There are some exceptions, however. For starters, if you're using the vehicle for personal conveyance, these rules don't apply to you. This is still a gray area to be honest. The authorities are mulling the introduction of another status called Yard Move which indicates a driver searching for a place to park their truck overnight and rest. The drivers' argument is that searching for a parking spot should count towards On Duty time, but this obviously doesn't make sense from a shipper's perspective.

In addition to the two-time windows mentioned previously, there are other time limits to adhere to. A driver cannot exceed a total of 70 hours spent in the On Duty or Driving statuses within an eight-day period. There's also another rule that specifies that once you move beyond eight hours from your previous 30-minute break (a break that lasts a minimum of 30 minutes), you must rest for at least 30 minutes in any status other than Driving.

FMCSA makes an exception for drivers who operate within 150 miles of their home base. In these cases, you might be allowed to maintain a time card instead of an eLD. However, given the direction in which technology is moving it's best to equip yourself with an ELD. Note that there are additional requirements to comply with before FMCSA will allow you to use a time card. You can find them at https://www.fmcsa.dot.gov/regulations/title49/part/395.

Here's where HOS rules get confusing. There is a situation or rule called the 8/2 Sleeper Split. 10 hours of rest are needed to reset the 14-hour On Duty window (and the 11-hour Driving window). These 10 hours can however be split into batches of eight and two hours each. Assuming you split your 14 hours this way, you can take a break for eight hours. Once your break is finished, you can resume driving and finish what was left of your larger window. If you drive for the majority of your 14-hour window, there isn't much of an issue with the rule.

However, let's say you drive for just two hours and then rest for eight hours for whatever reason. You now have nine hours out of 11 available to drive. Once you've driven those nine hours, FMCSA mandates that you need to rest for two hours at least. So, once you've rested for those two hours, you can get back up and drive another 11-hour window, right? Wrong! If you drive for 11 hours, this means you'll have driven for 20 hours on just two hours' worth of sleep. There's no way that's a safe situation.

FMCSA doesn't help matters by confusing everyone. They mandate that drivers must count the time spent driving after a partial rest against their current clock. Applying this to our previous example, the two hours driven before the partial rest is subtracted from the larger 11-hour window to give you nine hours of driving time. Pretty simple.

What if you drove for nine hours though? You now have two hours before taking a 10-hour break. This means you can drive for nine hours, rest for eight, drive for two and then rest for 10. This kind of split doesn't make any sense but it's the best we have. FMCSA further complicates matters by mandating that the partial rest periods can be taken in Sleeper or Off Duty status and splits can be taken in seven and three-hour batches as well.

All of this results in a massive headache for fleet managers and truck drivers. The best thing to do is to simply ignore all of these splits and drive for 11 hours and rest for 10. This makes life a lot easier for everyone and you won't need to worry about your compliance status. You can expect to be randomly inspected at truck stops by DoT inspectors who will check your ELD logs. If you're found in violation of HOS rules you will be fined and forced to rest until you're back in compliance again. Accumulate too many of these violations and you'll have problems acquiring insurance. So, keep it simple and don't bother with complicated splits. It makes planning your route much easier and you'll be able to indicate delivery times better to your customers.

Background Checks

FMCSA conducts thorough background checks on all owner-operators and drivers before providing them with a license. They take these checks very seriously so you should as well. The first step is a standard background check. Your motor vehicle record over the past three years will be scrutinized and all accident history or violations will be checked. Usually, this background check is carried out when you apply for your CDL and FMCSA will simply use that information to verify your credentials.

However, FMCSA might carry out random background checks. Red flags that they look for are alcohol or drug abuse. If you have a history of this without any rehab records, you can expect your application to be rejected.

Drug and alcohol tests are carried out routinely and randomly. You will have to subject yourself to a test when renewing your CDL. The DoT is the one that carries out random tests.

Here are the substances that drivers are specifically tested for (*Which substances are tested?*, 2020):

- Marijuana
- Cocaine
- Opiates
- Amphetamines and methamphetamines
- Phencyclidine

You cannot operate a vehicle if your blood alcohol level is over 0.02. If you're an independent owner-operator, DoT will carry out most inspections. However, if you're hired as part of a larger fleet by a carrier, you can expect them to carry out their independent tests before you can start working with them and they could test for drugs outside of the list above.

There are certain fixed points where drivers are always tested. For starters, you're tested before you receive your CDL. Next, you'll be tested if you're involved in an accident. There are exceptions to this rule. If you suffer bodily injury that requires immediate medical treatment away from the scene of the accident or if there's disabling damage to any vehicle that requires it to be towed away, you won't be tested at the scene. However, you will be tested either in the hospital/treatment facility or at the location where your vehicle is towed to. Owner-operators are expected to register with a consortium that manages all DOT drug and alcohol testing. These consortia typically have a network of labs, collection centers, and qualified medical officers who will supervise your tests. A typical consortium is a collection of participating owner-operators. The DOT supervises these consortia and requires them to conduct a fixed number of random drug tests throughout the year. Consortia have other powers as well. They have the ability to remove owner-operators from work if they fail a drug test or after any other violation. They will also assist the violating driver in their efforts to become compliant again. The Drug Alcohol Testing Industry Association (DATIA) has a directory that lists all drug testing consortiums in the country. DATIA also accredits various consortiums so it's an extremely reliable source. You can view DATIA's directories at https://www.datia.org/directories.html. Your choice of consortium is extremely important since it determines your overall compliance status with the DOT. You should choose one carefully. Many consortia have added services other than drug testing so make sure you evaluate all of them thoroughly. Something to look for is their prior experience administering drug testing programs. Ask them for referrals and for evidence of the quality of their service. They should also have good customer service to help you in case you have questions or need assistance of any kind. Make sure to obtain a phone number that has a real person behind it. A large network of collection centers helps since not every consortium has the facilities to collect testing samples all around the country.

So how often can you expect to be randomly tested? This depends on the rate that FMCSA mandates. You can check the rates at https://www.transportation.gov/odapc/random-testing-rates. You will be tested for drugs if there's a reasonable suspicion that you've been using them. This doesn't happen for owner-operators very often since physical observation is required. Typically, carrier drivers are subject to it more often since they have co-workers who can observe them at work. This doesn't mean it never happens to owner-operators so you should be wary.

The determination of reasonable suspicion is ambiguous and is up to the discretion of the consortium. If anyone in authority observes you behaving in a way that suggests you've drunk too much alcohol or consumed drugs, and if you're about to operate a vehicle, they will subject you to a test.

What happens if you fail a test? The DOT outlines strict return to duty criteria for all drivers. You will be expected to work with a DOT approved substance abuse professional who will certify your readiness to operate a truck. You will be placed under observation for a period of time before your test. The test itself is a driving test similar to your CDL test and will be directly observed by a DOT supervisor. Once you pass this test, you can return to active duty. Needless to say, you need a negative drug test before returning to duty.

The process doesn't end there. There are follow-up tests that are conducted over the course of a year. You will undergo at least six random drug tests. If you fail these tests or are not found to be in full compliance, this observation period can extend for up to four years, with six tests conducted every year.

The criteria for test failure is very clear. If you fail a drug test or if you register a blood alcohol level greater than 0.04, you will have failed. If you refuse to take a test, this counts as a failure as well. Medical conditions are valid reasons to opt out of a test.

However, the DOT specifies a fixed list of exceptions. You can view all of them at http://www.dot.gov/odapc/employee-handbook-english. Starting in 2021, all drivers are expected to register at the online drug and alcohol clearinghouse. This is an online repository that houses every driver's test results and history. Employers will use this database to conduct pre-employment checks. You should register at https://clearinghouse.fmcsa.dot.gov/.

That's all there is to drug testing. It's safe to say that you shouldn't operate a vehicle under the influence. You risk quite a lot and the authorities take a dim view of anyone violating these rules. Always comply with these requirements and you'll be just fine. Make sure you choose a good consortium that has robust processes that make it easy for you to submit samples and keep track of your results.

DVIRs

While drivers undergo extensive testing, the vehicles they operate are also subject to a number of tests. The DOT employs inspectors who conduct random inspection of vehicles at truck stops or even on the highway. While these random inspections don't inconvenience the driver too much, you shouldn't count on them occurring only when you're resting or at a stop. FMCSA mandates that drivers conduct a thorough inspection of their vehicle before they operate it. Drivers should also log inspection reports at the end of the day.

These reports are called Driver Vehicle Inspection Reports or DVIRs. They're an important part of your records so you should maintain them at all times. Any issues that are unearthed during your inspection should be dealt with before returning to the road. These days many ELD devices have the ability to monitor the status of your truck's internal machinery. They plug directly into your vehicle's computer and can access records. This makes inspection a lot easier.

However, there's a lot to be said for an old school eyeball check. DOT inspectors will use ELD logs but will also carry out physical inspections at weigh stations. If your vehicle weighs more than 10,000 pounds it will be inspected at least once every year.

The DOT outlines inspection procedures quite clearly. There are six inspection levels with the first level called the North American Standard Inspection (Mrozek, 2020).

This is the most comprehensive inspection that the DOT carries out. Inspectors will check all relevant documents that indicate the vehicle's roadworthiness including prior maintenance records.

They will also search for alcohol, drugs, and hazardous materials. At the very least, you should have your CDL, HOS logs, and DVIR logs on hand to give the inspectors.

The last two can be obtained from your ELD device and you can submit them electronically to the inspectors. This is still a relatively new way of doing things, so the process varies from one inspection to the next.

While one inspector looks at your logs, the other inspects your seatbelts, lights, wipers, cargo securing systems, tires, brakes, exhausts, fuel systems, emergency exits, frames, and coupling devices. The level one test lasts for a few hours at least. Typically, notice of these tests is provided in advance since they take so much time. You'll have to drive to a weigh station and have everything checked out. The level two test is similar to level one with the exception that any item that requires the inspector to dive under the truck will not be inspected. You will still need to provide all of your logs and paperwork.

While it isn't as exhaustive as the previous level, your vehicle should be in good shape if you wish to pass this test. The third level of inspection is carried out on the driver, instead of the vehicle.

There is a list of standard documents that the DOT will check. In no particular order, they are (Mrozek, 2020):

- Historical duty logs
- HOS logs
- CDL validity
- HAZMAT qualification if applicable
- Medical card
- Skill performance evaluations
- Seat belt condition
- Drug test records
- DVIRs

Next, we have the level four inspection. This is often called a special inspection and involves looking at a particular feature of your vehicle. The DOT inspector determines this, and these inspections are often used to collect data.

For example, if some manufacturers are found to have faulty suspensions (for example), the DOT inspector will examine this part of your truck. Most random inspections are usually level fours.

You might be asked to provide DVIR and HOS logs so keep them handy. Level five inspections are the same as level one inspections, except it's just the truck that is subject to an examination. In most cases, the driver is physically absent when these inspections are carried out.

A level five inspection is automatically carried out after an accident or a serious incident of some kind. The ELD devices of these vehicles are scrutinized so you will need to provide inspectors with access to those logs. Level six inspections are reserved for trucks that are transporting highly dangerous or radioactive materials.

They're level one inspections except they also contain material specific inspections. For example, the storage conditions and trailer loads are inspected to make sure the material is being transported safely.

Make sure you carry out regular proactive maintenance of your vehicle to avoid any last-minute surprises. You don't want to be discovering issues with your equipment right before the test. Often, issues arise when you're on the road and to deliver your load on time, you'll need to apply a hack to make sure you're able to fulfill your contract.

Don't let these hacks be anything more than short term solutions. Make sure you fix the faults in a timely manner so that you don't have to deal with larger issues down the road. Tires, brake systems, and couplings often fail on a truck so make sure you carry out proactive maintenance on them.

Maintain your DVIR log rigorously. Many freight brokers and shippers will ask to take a look at your logs to evaluate how reliable you are. They're not concerned with your vehicle's condition as much as they're looking at how disciplined you are when it comes to vehicle maintenance and compliance. The transportation industry revolves around compliance so it's important to fulfill the requirements you're responsible for.

HAZMAT Requirements

Due to their nature, hazardous materials are treated differently by FMCSA. You can read about the rules and regulations of transporting hazardous materials at https://www.fmcsa.dot.gov/regulations/title49/b/5/3/list?filter=HazMat.

While most owner-operators won't be transporting these materials, it's helpful to know them briefly. You need to register as a HAZMAT carrier in the United States to transport these loads. Your FMCSA application will contain a relevant section where you should indicate the loads you wish to carry.

All HAZMAT goods should be properly labeled, classed, described, and packaged. The penalties for violating these rules are huge. All workers who handle these materials should be properly trained and qualified to perform their duties. Refer to the link above to learn more about HAZMAT handling procedures.

Securing Cargo

Regular cargo must be secured according to procedures prescribed by FMCSA.

All tie-downs must be securely fastened. Chocks and wedges must be used to prevent rolling. FMCSA uses a standard formula to determine how many tie-downs must be used depending on the weight of the cargo.

Objects that are five feet or less in length and less than 1,100 lbs must have at least one tie down. Objects greater than this must have at least two tie-downs.

Objects that require special tie down procedures aren't subject to these regulations and you should follow their specific needs. When loading your truck make sure that it doesn't obscure your front or side views.

There shouldn't be any packaging issues and all cargo must be securely enclosed within their packages.

Your tie-downs and cargo securement systems should be able to withstand 0.8g deceleration forward, 0.5g backwards and to the side. You can view a detailed description of cargo securing requirements at https://www.fmcsa.dot.gov/regulations/cargo-securement/cargo-securement-rules.

CSA Program

CSA comes under FMCSA's large rulebook but it's an important portion and deserves its own section. CSA stands for Compliance,

Safety, and Accountability and is aimed at increasing road safety and the safety of the operators of commercial vehicles. High-risk carriers are removed from the roads and are identified by abnormal CSA scores. These scores are calculated by taking into account the number of safety incidents you've had since your CDL was issued.

CSA scores are assigned on a percentile basis. The lower the score is, the safer a carrier is. For example, if one percent of all carriers have had less than 20 incidents throughout the previous year, those one percent are the lowest percentile and have the highest CSA score.

These scores are stored in the Safety Measurement System or SMS. As roadside inspections are carried out every month, the SMS is updated with fresh scores.

The SMS scores all drivers on seven elements. These are the Behavior Analysis and Safety Improvement Categories (BASICs). These categories are (*FMCSA Regulations: A Guide for Fleet Managers*, 2020):

- Unsafe driving - Speeding, not wearing a seatbelt, improper lane changes, etc.
- Crash indicator - Historical crash patterns and severity of crashes
- HOS compliance

- Vehicle maintenance or DVIRs
- Drug and alcohol testing records
- HAZMAT compliance
- Driver fitness - Does the driver have a valid license, medical card, and paperwork indicating their qualifications?

DOT inspectors evaluate every trucker according to these categories and score them respectively. These individual scores are added together to provide the overall CSA score. Remember that the scores are assigned on a scale of one to ten, but the overall CSA score is graded according to a percentile. The lower the percentile is, the better a trucker's score is. A score of 20 and below is considered great. It indicates the trucker is amongst the top 20 percent of all carriers in the country. All of the BASICs have thresholds that upon violation, result in automatic inspections. Typically, HOS compliance, unsafe driving, and crash indicators have a high correlation with road safety. These categories have low thresholds and FMCSA is particularly sensitive about these BASICs. HAZMAT thresholds are also low, usually lower than the ones I just mentioned. These thresholds are usually fixed at 65% although an inspector has the power to initiate inspection for lower scores as well. HAZMAT thresholds are fixed at 60%. The other BASICs have a relatively high threshold of 80%. You might be wondering how all of these scores affect you? What I mean is, road safety is important and everything, but will it impact you financially? It turns out they will. Your CSA score is the first thing an insurer will look at before offering you a premium. The higher your CSA score is, the greater is your insurance premium. If you have repeatedly exceeded thresholds, you can expect to pay a huge amount in insurance premiums.

Obtaining low CSA scores isn't difficult if you drive safely, maintain meticulous records, and pass your inspections. Many truckers think of ways to rig their CSA scores or try to figure out flaws they can exploit in the system. It's far easier to simply do the right thing and to be as safe as possible on the roads. This is the best way to guarantee a good safety score.

IFTA Reporting

Something that truckers need to worry about uniquely in the logistics industry is IFTA reporting. IFTA, as you've already learned, stands for International Fuel Tax Agreement and this standardizes a lot of the fuel tax reporting requirements that many states used to have. In the past, each state had its own unique method of reporting and this created a ton of confusion, not to mention paperwork. IFTA solves that problem and the process is a lot simpler now.

Thanks to IFTA, motor carriers that operate in multiple states require to file just one fuel tax return every quarter in their home jurisdiction. Home jurisdiction here refers to the state where you reside, not where your LLC is formed. Prior to IFTA, carriers had to obtain individual fuel permits from every state they wished to transit through. These days, you receive a single IFTA license and decals that you will need to renew every year.

Renewing your license and decal is as simple as paying the fees as explained in the earlier chapter about permits. IFTA applies to the lower 48 states and 10 Canadian provinces in North America. The report you file lists the amount of money you owe or the refund you're due every quarter. Many truckers think the IFTA tax filing process is complicated but once you grasp the basics it's pretty straightforward. You might find your first filing a bit of a headache but it's smooth sailing from there on out. The Department of Revenue has an online portal that allows you to complete your IFTA fuel tax returns. In addition to this, each state has an online portal that allows you to enter your information online and determine your fuel tax obligations. There are a few subtleties you should be aware of when filing the IFTA return.

Base State

This is one of the most confusing aspects of IFTA. Technically, a trucking company that operates across multiple states, with customers in all of them or deliveries in each state can register any of those places as its base state. IFTA doesn't specify the requirements for a base state. Some truckers choose to elect the state their LLC is incorporated in as their base state. Some choose their state of residence as I mentioned previously. The choice is yours at the end of the day. You will encounter a lot of talk about a high fuel state versus a low fuel state. It can get pretty confusing when you dive into such detail. As a rule of thumb, your base state should be the one where your motor vehicle is registered or is largely operational. Your paperwork will become much easier to file when you do it this way. Don't worry about taxes, they'll take care of themselves. The amount of money you'll save registering in a low or high fuel tax state isn't worth the amount of time you'll spend staying compliant.

If you're running a large fleet, it's best to speak to a CPA to discuss registration basics. If you have more than 10 trucks, registering in a low tax state might have huge advantages for you. However, below this number, it isn't as significant.

Qualified Vehicles

A qualified IFTA vehicle is one that travels between at least two jurisdictions. It must weigh over 26,000 pounds or have three or more axles. The qualified vehicle must use diesel, propane, or natural gas. Note that some states allow gas-powered vehicles to register themselves as well. It's pretty rare to find a big rig that is gas-powered, though.

The IFTA decal is tied to your vehicle, not to your FMCSA number or any other registration you possess. This means if you operate a fleet of more than one vehicle, you need to register each vehicle for IFTA compliance. These decals must be renewed every year at your local DMV, in your base state. You must also ensure that each vehicle carries a valid copy of your IFTA registration. Not displaying the IFTA decal on your vehicle will lead you to be pulled over by the cops if your tags don't match the state you're operating in. The penalties for this are huge so it isn't worth the risk.

Reporting

At the end of each calendar quarter, you must file a fuel tax report with the Secretary of your base state, and more importantly, you must include a check for the amount you owe. It is possible to be eligible for a refund, but this typically doesn't happen. If you receive a refund, it won't be as cash but as credit against future payments. The first quarter's due date is April 30th, Q2's is July 31st, Q3's is October 31st, and Q4's is January 31st of the following year. To file a report, you need to first register with the IFTA tax filing portal in your base state. You can find this link by searching for "your home state" + IFTA portal online. Registration is straightforward, and once this is done, you can log in to the portal to file your return.

You will need to enter your business' details such as the name, EIN, address, etc. When registering for the first time, you will be prompted to pick a base state. This state will show up when you login the next time. You'll then enter vehicle details, such as license plate number, make, model, and so on. Remember that you need to file the report for each vehicle on your company's books. The next section is the most important bit. You'll have to enter your distance and fuel records as recorded in your ELD. The ELD is the most accurate but you can also use GPS records or trip sheets if you maintain them. You'll need to enter your fuel purchases according to your receipts. To calculate the taxes you owe, you'll need to take a look at the IFTA fuel tax rates that are published at the following link: https://www.iftach.org/taxmatrix4/choose_tableqnew.php. If your state's online system is too confusing you can use third-party services such as Webfile, ExpressTruckTax, or EDI to help you calculate the taxes you owe and file online.

Receipts

You must include copies of your receipts with your electronic filing. All receipts must include the date of purchase, fuel type, seller's name, address, purchaser's name, vehicle registration, amount of sale, and the number of gallons of fuel purchased. You must also maintain vehicle mileage reports that must be summarized monthly.

Tips for Easy IFTA Reporting

As you can see there's a lot of paperwork that goes into IFTA reporting. This is one of those tasks that is best handled by an employee, especially if you're running a fleet. It's pretty tough for a single owner-operator to file IFTA for a single truck without having some sort of process to back them up. The best way to approach the quarterly filing is to do it proactively.

Many truckers collect their records at the last minute and try to figure out their taxes for the entire quarter at once. This process takes many hours and it can be hellish if you misplace receipts or can't locate proper vehicle logs. Instead, record your fuel purchases and receipts, along with trip logs, after every trip or every purchase. Many states' online systems allow you to save your records as you go. If you opt to use a third-party service you can easily enter your numbers and let the software take care of the tax calculator for you, throughout the quarter. Maintain meticulous receipts and vehicle mileage logs. These are the most important pieces of information in your filing and without them, you'll find it hard to justify anything you file. Always keep your receipts in paper as well as in digital format. Once you pay for fuel, make it a habit to take a picture of it and save it onto an online storage system. Alternatively, you can send it to your employee and have them store it and file the information on it. The key is to design a simple process that is repeatable and easily understood. Don't let your receipts pile up since this will only create more headaches for you down the road. As I mentioned in a previous chapter, designing processes is the key to running a successful business.

Other Compliance Requirements

While FMCSA and IFTA form the majority of your compliance reporting requirements, there are other small reports you'll need to file. These are annual compliance reports regarding your LLC and your tax return. Your tax return can be filed by a qualified CPA and this is a straightforward task if you hire the right person. Your LLC's annual compliance report depends on the state you form your company in. Some states have more detailed requirements than others. However, in most cases, your registered agent will do this for you and there's nothing you need to do yourself. If you choose to do it yourself, you should inquire about the process with the secretary of the state you've incorporated in.

As I mentioned earlier, it's best to focus on tasks you're good at and enjoy and hire out the ones you don't. These two tasks are certainly amongst the ones you want to hire out.

Chapter 8:
Finding Loads and Advertising Yourself - Part One

O nce you've gone through the full registration process, set up your company, and completed all the other formalities you need to complete, it can be easy to think you're on the threshold of making huge amounts of money. However, this is just the beginning. Marketing and finding work is what drives your business forward and you need to execute these tasks perfectly to grow your business. Marketing scares many truckers since it seems intimidating. After all, mention the word marketing and the first thing that comes to mind is a suit walking around Madison Avenue. This seems the farthest thing from what a trucker ought to be. The truth is that these days marketing is a must-have for all businesses. There are so many channels that grab people's attention. You have to market yourself if you want to successfully attract customers to you. The good news is that all of these channels are easily accessible, and you can leverage all of them to find great work. As I mentioned previously, the best work is often unadvertised. If you're stuck on load boards searching for work, you're probably not executing marketing tactics very well. Many truckers find themselves in this position because they're either ignorant of the online world or are so intimidated by it that they choose to ignore it completely.

Marketing can be intimidating but it's solved by implementing a simple process. In this chapter I'm going to walk you through all of the options you have available and help you implement a simple process that you can execute. You can choose to use all of the channels I highlight or just a few. There's no rule that says you have to be present in every single channel I mention here. Above all else, remember that other truckers are your friends. They're the ones who will pass work they can't fulfill onto you and you can lean on them to handle loads you can't fulfill and still keep a customer happy. Networking is what drives the logistics industry and trucking is no different. Before we dive into the different aspects of marketing, let's take some time to explore an important topic. This concerns your niche. Your niche is the category into which you've chosen to slot yourself. It can be defined by the loads you haul, the type of equipment you choose to run, or even the locations you choose to operate in. For example, you could be hauling timber out of Oregon to California or you could be short-hauling oil around Texas. It's important for you to clearly define your niche before you begin your trucking business. A niche helps you stand out as an expert or as a trustworthy business owner. Think about it. If you were in the market to buy cologne for yourself, would you head over to a general store that sells everything or would you trust a cologne store more? The latter has clearly defined their niche and dominates it. You must do the same. Many truckers choose to haul everything in sight, and this makes them a jack of all trades. They end up knowing a little of everything but fail to build deep relationships since they're too busy hauling loads for little money. Such truckers remain on load boards for their entire careers and never make the step up.

Pick a niche that is relevant to your local area or state and stick to it.

It'll help you dive deep into that industry and you'll make better connections. When a customer that ships timber needs help, they're not going to call the guy that ships everything. They'll call the person who hauls timber and nothing else. They know that this person knows their product and how to store it and deliver it safely.

Niching yourself also simplifies your marketing since it's easier to focus and target your ideal customer. It helps you narrow your focus and get more lucrative work before those listings ever hit load boards. So how can you begin marketing yourself? It all begins with one of the most fundamental business assets you can own.

The First Step

The first step you need to take in your marketing plan is to have a website. In the earlier portion of the previous decade, businesses could get away with not having an online presence. People were still wary of online gimmicks and social media hadn't become the behemoth it is today. However, consumers these days are well educated with regard to online purchases and trust the online buying process much more. They're not as skeptical about what they see on a website. Most consumers search for a person online before they meet them in person. If you're recommended to someone by an existing customer, the first thing that person does is Google you. If you have a professional-looking social media profile and a good website, they'll naturally feel as if you're a serious business person. If nothing about you shows up online, it's as if you don't truly exist.

Invest in a good website and you'll reap the rewards. Besides giving you credibility, a good website also helps you stand out more. Most truckers don't bother with a website or even with marketing. They don't have any way of communicating with prospective customers and rely on infrequent recommendations or simply get lucky. Be smarter than these people and get yourself a professional-looking website.

Building a Website

Building a website these days is much easier than you think. There are a number of platforms that allow you to create a fully functional website in less than a couple of hours. WordPress is the most popular option. Other options include Wix and Squarespace. You can sign up with these platforms and create a free website. However, the free website will have their brands on it so it's not the most professional choice. You'll also be limited in the amount of marketing you can carry out online. The best choice is to sign up for a professional website. You'll need to buy a domain through these platforms and design your website. A simple two-page website is more than enough for your needs as a trucker. You can invest more money and have someone design it for you, but this isn't strictly necessary. One page on your website should list information about yourself and the services you provide. The second page should have a contact form where people can get in touch with you. Make sure you include testimonials from satisfied customers on your website. All website building platforms have plugins or software that allow you to drag and drop testimonial sections. You can then enter what your customers have said about you as text into these sections and your website will be ready to go. In terms of costs, a website is next to nothing. A domain will cost you around $15 at the most while hosting and website service plans will cost you around $20 per month. This is the price you'll pay if you choose Wix or Squarespace. They manage everything for you. If you choose WordPress, you'll need to choose your own hosting and connect everything yourself. This isn't particularly difficult to do but if you aren't computer savvy it can lead to some headaches. It is cheaper, but since you can cut costs more. Once your website is up, make sure to get yourself a professional email address. You can do this through the website building platform itself. Don't rely on a Gmail address. Compare these two addresses: trucking@gmail.com versus john@instantrrucking.com. Which one looks more professional? The answer is obvious. You can sign up with Google for a business address for as low as $6 per month. Link your business email address to your website, if the platform doesn't do this automatically, and you're good to go. You have a great base from which you can build your marketing plans.

Design Tips

You'll be creating a pretty simple website, but this doesn't mean you should invest minimal effort into it. While it won't make or break your business, you do want to present a professional look to your prospective clients. Everyone's going to be checking it out to evaluate you so it's crucial that you follow a few simple design tips. For starters, have a good picture of yourself on there. This is your company's website and people will want to know who they're doing business with. Have a friend take a professional looking photo of yourself. You don't have to wear a suit and tie since this would look incongruous on a trucker. However, a few pictures of you posing next to your rig is appropriate. Explain how you'll solve your client's problems on your website. Many business owners start talking about themselves, but your website should be all about problem-solving. Your customers are coming to you because they have issues. Tell them how you'll solve it. Use testimonials to highlight how you'll solve these issues. For example, delayed loads are a common issue. Explain how great your record is and accentuate the positives.

Don't be shy about asking for testimonials. Always make it a point to ask people to write you a few words of praise and get their permission to use their name and job title on your website. Prospective customers rely on customer reviews to make buying decisions. You should use this to the fullest. It's also a good idea to link your business address to a Google Maps pin.

This will allow your customers to leave you Google reviews. When anyone searches for you on Google, these reviews will pop up on the right-hand side of the screen (much like they do when you search for a restaurant), and you'll build credibility. Make sure your contact form is clear and always capture the full name and email of the person who fills out your form. You can use their emails down the road, and I'll explain this marketing tactic. Keep the colors and fonts on your website clean and simple. Don't get carried away with animation or pop-ups. It just annoys people and makes you look unprofessional.

If bootstrapping your costs isn't an issue you can invest in a logo designer and hire someone to design your website. Again, this won't make or break your business but it's a nice way of presenting a professional profile to your prospective clients.

Blog Marketing

All websites these days come equipped with a blog. A blog is a great way for you to attract clients to yourself. It takes a while but it's worth it over the long run. A blog will help you get found on Google. Creating content for a blog is tough and most truckers will balk at having to write anything online. However, thanks to the way Google works these days, you don't have to write anything. YouTube is a great way to create video content that replicates a blog. Your videos don't have to be movie quality either. All you need to do is talk about the issues that are relevant to hauling loads. Upload these to a YouTube channel (free) and embed those same videos on your blog. Google has the ability to read video content and will link to your video in Google's search results. Creating a video is as simple as recording yourself on a smartphone. The question is what should you talk about? You'll hear a lot of talk about using keyword research tools and other software that help you reverse engineer Google's algorithm and so on. None of this is necessary. In fact, all you need is to look at Google's search results. To be precise, you need to search for topics related to your niche and then look at the search suggestions that Google provides at the bottom of the page. Google also provides a list of questions in the middle of the page that you can use to decide what kind of content you want to create. If writing really isn't your thing, then record a six-minute video that talks about this topic and post it on YouTube. You won't get much traction at first but if you're consistent, you'll begin to see results within a year or so. A year sounds like a long time, but remember that you're in this for the long-term. Your aim with your blog is to keep your business relevant for the next 10 years, not just the next few months. A well-maintained blog or YouTube channel will help you do this. The key is to remain consistent. You should look to upload videos or release blog articles once every week. Maintain this schedule over the long term and you'll manage to attract traffic from Google.

The great thing about this method is that once you put in the initial effort, your blog is always present on the web. It will continue to attract traffic as long as your content is relevant.

Using Social Media

Social media is everywhere these days and the lines between online and offline worlds have blurred. Leveraging the right social media tools is crucial if you want to market yourself successfully. There are many social media platforms these days and the question is, which ones should you focus on? Given that your objective is to build a professional profile, LinkedIn is a no-brainer. In addition to LinkedIn, Facebook is also a great choice. The other social media platforms aren't quite as useful. In fact, as time moves on even Facebook is becoming less relevant. However, it's a good place to start.

Facebook

Facebook is a great way to network with other truckers and shippers in your area or even nationally. There are a ton of groups that are dedicated to sourcing loads and connecting shippers with truckers. Note that a Facebook group is unlikely to give you a steady stream of work. In fact, most groups are populated by truckers looking for work and very few shippers. Think of it as a low-quality load board. So why should you spend time on these boards?

Simply put, networking. Facebook groups offer tremendous networking opportunities and you'll get to meet a lot of truckers who are in a similar line of work as yours. Also, you never know when someone might have a requirement and you can land work on these groups.

Just don't make them your only source of work. Here's a list of some of the best Facebook groups for truckers:

- Truck driving jobs in the US and Canada
- Truck drivers of the US and Canada
- CDL truck driver JOBS
- Truckersreport.com Trucking Forum

These groups are focused on job listings. However, there are other groups that aren't dedicated to finding jobs but attract a lot of truckers to them. Some of these groups are:

- Truck repair services in US and Canada
- Trucks for sale
- Truck products

- Truckin' Runners
- Big truck health and fitness
- Driven to be healthy

These groups have a ton of lively discussion and are a great way to network and meet with other truckers in your area, or wherever you'll be driving to. While their primary purpose isn't to list loads, a lot of business takes place via private messaging once you build a relationship with some of the other people in these groups. Aim to provide value in these groups and don't spam people with messages inquiring about loads. These groups are also a great way to build a support network for your business. You'll find many finance firms, mechanics, and towing service professionals in them. The support of these people is essential to help you tide over short term difficulties you might have. For example, if you've broken down in a remote area, it's nice to have someone to contact who can put you in touch with a reliable service provider who can have you up and running quickly.

LinkedIn

When it comes to business networking, there's no better social network than LinkedIn. This platform doesn't get much advertising but B2B professionals know its value. B2B stands for business to business and it's what the trucking industry is. After all, you're providing services to other businesses, not individuals. LinkedIn is a very different platform from Facebook in terms of the tone people adopt. It's the online equivalent of your resume so you can imagine how you need to treat it. Keep your political and religious beliefs to yourself and remain professional. Talk about your services and always seek to provide value. The great thing about LinkedIn is that you can directly get in touch with customers and shippers in your target companies. Before you begin using LinkedIn, take some time to make a list of companies in your area that you would like to target. Obviously, these companies need to be in your niche. Do some research on them and find out whether they have internal logistics teams or whether they work with a dedicated carrier. You can search LinkedIn for clues as well. Search for the company and then take a look at their employee roster. If you find the words "logistics" or "shipping" in any of their job titles, you're in luck. It means they have an internal team that handles all shipments. They might be working with a dedicated carrier, but this doesn't mean you should ignore them. Create a professional looking profile that mirrors your website. You can literally copy-paste text from your site to your profile. LinkedIn allows you to define your job title so make sure you use relevant descriptions on there. For example, don't use something like "truckin' hauls daily" to describe what you do. Instead use phrases like "owner-operator" or "truck owner" as your job title.

The reason is that customers will search for these terms when they look for truckers. If you want to appear in their search results, you need to use relevant terms. Your profile also needs to contain relevant terms that indicate to LinkedIn's algorithm that you're in the trucking industry. If you've used text from your website this shouldn't be a problem. Paste a link to your website on your profile so that people can access it easily. LinkedIn allows you to upload a cover photo on your profile. Upload an image that contains your email address and phone number so that people can easily get in touch with you. Staying active on LinkedIn is important. Like with Facebook, LinkedIn has a bunch of groups that are actively geared towards the transportation industry.

LinkedIn's groups as a gold mine for networking with professionals in the industry. Here are a few examples of groups that are popular:

- A Truckload, Trucking, Logistics, Supply Chain, 3PL, Distribution group. Transportation, Transport
- Transportation Network for Freight Brokers, Logistics, Supply Chain, Carrier Trucking Professionals
- American Trucking Association
- Women In Trucking Association, Inc
- Trucking Insiders Circle
- Truck Driver and Trucking Forum
- Customers Seeking Best Trucking Carriers

These groups are far more reliable than the ones on Facebook since everyone on here has a professional profile and is verified in one way or another. Not only will you have access to truckers and customers, but you'll also get to network with other professionals such as freight brokers and carriers. These connections are invaluable if you want to attract the best loads to yourself. The key is to promote yourself as someone who brings a ton of value to the table. Remember those video blogs you'll create for your website? Well, share those videos on here and seek feedback from group members. You'll come across as someone who is knowledgeable and is professional. People will begin to see you as an authority even if you aren't the most experienced. One of the things you should do when you join a group is to add everyone in it as a connection. Send them a connection request with a short introductory message. People are very open to connecting with one another on LinkedIn, so this is perfectly fine. Once you've connected with people, LinkedIn allows you to view the other person's contact information. This will be either an email or an email with a phone number. If you're comfortable, you can cold call this person to check whether they have any leads for you. However, it's far better to save their email and to use it in the way I'll describe down the road. Keep connecting with as many relevant people as possible and keep engaging within your groups. I'll show you later how to create a marketing task schedule that will help you execute all of your tasks easily. For now, just understand that all you need to do is dedicate 30 minutes daily to networking on LinkedIn.

Forums

Website forums were perhaps the first type of social media platforms that existed. While most people don't hang around on forums anymore, in the trucking industry forums are quite popular. There are a number of close-knit online communities of truckers who you can network with. In fact, if you're active on the two social media platforms I just highlighted, you'll find many familiar faces on these forums. This is a good thing since you'll only become more popular in the community. Here are some of the most popular forums for truckers:

- Team run smart - This website also has an active Facebook group
- Truckers report

- Trucking truth
- The truckers forum
- Class A drivers
- Expeditersonline.com

These aren't the only trucking forums out there. However, they are probably the most active and the best for networking. Your approach on these forums should be the same as on social media. Always give value and don't bombard people with requests for loads. That's not going to give you any results. Instead, be an active member of the community and always give help as much as possible. You'll slowly find members reaching out to you for jobs they can't handle or leads they'd like to pass onto you. Make sure you do the same for others as well and you'll build a network that brings you steady work.

When put together, social media has the power to bring you a steady line of work. You never know where your next load will come from so always be active. Spend a little time every day responding to comments and posting on these channels and you'll build a solid reputation. LinkedIn is probably the best resource for you, but never ignore the power of forums.

Posting and commenting on other people's posts is a routine part of any social media marketing effort. There are more active methods that you should carry out. These methods will boost traffic to your website and will bring you more leads.

Online Marketing Methods

In this subchapter, I'm going to give you a few methods that will help you tie your online effort together. Thus far, you've learned that you need to build a website and network on social media. You've also learned that collecting emails is important. You're now going to learn how you can collect even more emails and how you can use them.

Collecting Emails

LinkedIn connections are a great way to get access to people's emails. However, not everyone you message on the platform is going to connect with you. People have busy lives and aren't keen on spending too much time networking on social media. So how can you collect these people's emails and stay in touch with them?

There are a variety of online tools that help you do this. Perhaps the best tool is Hunter.io. The way to use this tool is to enter the website address of the company your prospect works for and then enter their name. The tool then returns the most probable format of their official email address.

Here's how you can execute this step by step. First, open your prospect's LinkedIn profile. If they haven't connected with you as yet, click on their company's page. The company page will have a link to the company website. Copy the URL, and paste it into Hunter's "finder" tab. Next, enter your prospect's name (from their LinkedIn profile) into the relevant box in Hunter and click "find". You'll receive the email address. Collecting emails like this is great but what do you do with them? There are two ways to go about using these emails. The first is to cold email these prospects. The second is to try to warm them up before pitching them your services. Between the two, the second option has a far higher success rate. The first option works but it might come across as being too intrusive.

Send your prospect an email introducing yourself but don't ask for work. Instead, tell them that you'd like to interview them about a relevant topic for your blog or YouTube channel. You'll find people far more responsive when you do this since you're not asking them for a favor. Set up a time to interview them and throughout the interview, position yourself as an owner-operator who knows a lot about your niche.

Once you're done conducting the informational interview, send them a copy of the transcript and ask them whether they need any changes. Once you've made changes, publish it and send them the link. Along with the link, tell them that you'd like to remain in touch with them and would like to do so through your email newsletter. I'll shortly describe how to set up a newsletter. Not every prospect is going to respond to your interview request. In fact, most of them won't respond. This isn't a bad sign. In fact, most people are extremely busy and might want to respond but forget to do so given the mountain of tasks in front of them. Send them a follow-up email after a week and another a week later, up to three times. In your final, third follow-up email, mention that you'd like to stay in touch with them via your newsletter and that they can unsubscribe whenever they like. This is a slightly aggressive way of getting people onto your mailing list but as long as you give them the option to unsubscribe, it's fine.

The beauty of this method is that you'll build your reputation in the industry by creating great content with people who are active within it. This also solves your problem of having to think of new ideas for content. It puts you in front of people who will ultimately hire you (potentially) and you can build relationships with them without coming across as desperate for work. Most truckers don't do this and stick to tired old marketing methods. The result is that while a few get lucky, most end up going back to working for a carrier. The online world is teeming with opportunities and you're leaving money on the table if you aren't active in it. Once you've collected someone's email, you need to start running a newsletter for them.

Email Newsletters

Emails are an extremely valuable asset for any sales team. While social media and paid ads garner all the media attention, the good old email is still the most valuable piece of information you can obtain about a person. Running a newsletter is a really easy task. Best of all, it's automated. Your website platform will have an option that allows you to create a newsletter and enter the email addresses to which you want to send them. Creating the newsletter itself is straightforward. You can choose from a set of pre-designed templates. Make sure you choose one that looks professional and matches the overall tone and design of your website. Within the newsletter, you should highlight one of your latest pieces of content and leave a link back to your website and your LinkedIn profile. You can include other sections where you curate content that is related to your industry. You can highlight other people's articles or trade publication articles and so on. Make sure you leave links in the newsletter to your YouTube channel as well if you're creating video content. Don't make your newsletter lengthy. Your prospects should be able to read all of it within a single scroll.

Run your newsletter to your prospects once a month. Your platform will give you the ability to view analytics on your newsletter campaigns. You'll be able to view how many people opened your newsletter and how many clicked on the links within it. If you're receiving a large number of opens and clicks, increase the frequency to twice a month (once every other week) and see how your metrics hold up.

Ultimately, you can't force people to hire you. They'll come to you when they have a need for your services. So, keep running your newsletter and keep growing your email list. Over time, you'll begin to notice that people will start sending you inquiries and you'll land jobs. The best part about this is you'll be able to farm out these jobs to other people. After a while, your pipeline will be full enough for you to contemplate starting your own fleet. Building a successful marketing engine takes time but it's worth every second you invest in it. Don't expect short term results through these methods. You can expect it to take anywhere from three months to a year to begin bearing fruit. Of course, I'm not implying you should starve in the meantime. You can always find loads on load boards and through other marketing tactics I'll discuss in the next chapter.

However, make sure you set up your online marketing engine properly since it's automated. Once it begins rolling and gains traction, it'll bring you jobs that the average trucker won't have access to since they won't be advertised.

A significant portion of successful marketing is combining multiple methods to bring you success. In the next chapter, I'm going to give you some of the other methods that work very well.

Chapter 9:
Finding Loads and Advertising Yourself - Part Two

I n the previous chapter, you learned all about online marketing and how you need to present a professional persona of your business. The thing with online marketing as outlined in that chapter is that it takes time. Once it gets rolling, you're all good.

What do you do in the interim while you're still building momentum? It's not as if you should simply sit around doing nothing.

There are many tactics you can use to drive interest toward yourself. The most obvious one is using paid social media ads. Most people opt for Facebook ads, but it really isn't a good fit for truckers.

Think about it. It's unlikely that a logistics manager at a client or a shipper is browsing Facebook looking for truckers.

They're probably on there to destress and look at cat videos. Trucking is the last thing on their mind.

Google ads are the best online advertising option for you. This is because people directly search for trucking services in their local area on Google and your ads will drive people to visit your website and contact you. The thing with online ads is that they cost money. Online ads work on a cost per click model. This means you'll pay money whenever people click your ad. There's no guarantee of landing a load and you'll be spending money the entire time waiting for someone to contact you. If you have the budget and aren't too concerned about bootstrapping, feel free to run online ads.

Google's Keyword tool within its Ad Manager is an extremely useful resource that will help you determine which keywords to advertise for. Target keywords that have a search volume of at least 1,000 per month.

Setting up a Google ads account and ads is pretty straightforward. If money is a concern for you then you're going to have to resort to offline methods.

These methods are some of the most popular ones amongst truckers since they typically don't use online tactics.

You'll likely find a lot of competition by doing this, but your online presence will help you stand out. Let's look at some of these methods now.

Offline Marketing Tactics

The world has changed immeasurable to the point where these "offline" tactics used to be "primary" marketing tactics.

The good news for you is that most of the trucking world hasn't moved on from them so you'll be better positioned once you enter the field. The most prevalent method of finding clients is to cold call them.

Cold Calling

Cold calling as a sales tactic is used in pretty much every industry. The premise is simple. You find someone's contact information and call them and hope they don't hang up on you. It's a brute force tactic and is entirely a numbers game. Many books have been written about it but ultimately, it comes down to how well you can take rejection and how well you can source contact information. Sourcing phone numbers to call is the toughest part of cold calling. you can poke around local phone number registries but the best way to introduce yourself is to physically visit them on their work premises. You can drive to the closest local carrier or shipper and ask to be introduced to the manager. Typically, these companies expect truckers to visit them, so they won't be hostile to your visit.

Make sure you have printed business cards (with your website address) on you to give them. You'll need to pitch them your services in a quick and concise manner. Here's a sample script you can use: "Hi <<their name>>, I'm <<your name>> from <<your company's name>>. We've been working with some companies in your area like <<companies just like theirs>> and I wanted to introduce myself to you"

Ask them a few questions about their current shipping setup and whether they're looking to change trucking companies or whether they're dissatisfied with some portion of the process. More often than not, you'll receive an objection. They'll likely say that they already work with one of your competitors and that they aren't looking for a change.

This is a perfectly fine response. Tell them that you understand. Instead of trying to sling mud on their current service provider, highlight your positive qualities instead. Talk about your excellent customer service or your experience. Talk about how you'll guarantee their loads arrive on time and how you always follow the highest levels of compliance.

Leave with their email address and phone number (usually on their business card) and add that person to your newsletter campaign. Make sure you tell them that you'd like to remain in touch with them through a newsletter that has helpful information about the trucking industry. If the prospect tells you that they aren't interested, use the same response and simply add them to your email newsletter. It costs them nothing to give you a work email so add them to your list and move on. If you're wondering where you can find business listings of shippers in your area, the best place to check is with other truckers. You can also search online for shippers in your locality. If there is a huge factory nearby you can bet that they need truckers to move their equipment.

LinkedIn is also a great way of figuring out which companies operate in your area. You can search by geography on the platform and locate local companies. There are paid options such as Zoominfo and LeadIRO but these databases cost a lot of money. If you're planning on scaling your business to a large fleet right off the bat you can use these. You can also use MacRae's Blue Book and The Industry 500 to locate potential shippers in your area. If you're in the agricultural niche, you can use the USDA's business listings to find local shippers. A non-traditional option is to use Google's satellite view. You can scour your area for commercial buildings that have loading docks.

Google will likely have a pin that lists the address and the company's name. These places could be customers potentially. Lastly, you can take a look at load boards and find local listings on there. Even if you don't land a load, you can always visit the listing agent and get in touch with them. Another variation of the cold calling method is to cold email prospects. As I mentioned in the previous chapter, this is a brute force approach and is quite impersonal. You might get lucky once in a while but it's better to call your prospects or visit them in person.

Trade Shows

Trade shows and conferences are a goldmine for truckers. You'll find many trucking and logistics providers at these shows trying to drum up some business. Before the COVID-19 pandemic hit, most trade shows provided ample opportunities for organic networking. You'd start chatting to someone next to you and exchange business cards in the hope of networking with one another. These days, the organic meeting dynamic has changed thanks to events moving online. Some online events have networking booths where people can "speed network" with one another but it isn't quite the same. However, this doesn't mean you should neglect to attend these conferences. Some conferences will charge you money to attend but most of them are free. One of the benefits of attending conferences online is that you can quickly take a look at the event sponsors and access their website and LinkedIn pages. This gives you quick access to the emails and contact information of their employees. If they're a good fit for your niche, you can quickly add them to your newsletter strategy and start marketing to them. Within the event itself, a lot depends on how the show is structured. All events have keynote speakers but look at the list of attendees as well. Usually, these conferences will display the emails of the people that are attending the event. You can figure out which companies they work for by looking at their emails. For example, "john_doe@xyzcorp.com" clearly works for XYZ Corp. The ".com" appendage also indicates their website address. Type it into your browser and take a look at what they do. If it's a match for your business, you can start bringing them into your online marketing methods. Eventually, conferences will move back to an in-person format but until then you'll need an online strategy to back your networking up. In-person formats are far easier to figure out. You can make small talk with other attendees. It's helpful to prepare a few flyers or brochures that describe what you do, however this isn't necessary. It simply saddles people with marketing material that they're likely to throw away once the event ends. Instead, create good business cards with relevant contact information on them. Prepare an elevator pitch that describes what you do. For example, "We're a logistics solutions provider for <<your preferred type of company/product/niche>>. We operate out of <<your location>>. Here's our information <<hand them card>>". Keep your introduction short and to the point. Don't launch into a detailed description of how wonderful your rig is or the specifics of the routes you run. Most people won't be interested in that.

One of the keys to enhancing your networking relationships is to ask questions. Conferences are places where you can really stand out by doing this. Most people are there to network and are completely focused on promoting themselves. They're in a rush to describe what they do and pitch themselves. This can leave the other person feeling a bit let down. Turn this on its head by asking them what they do and asking them questions about it.

Of course, you don't want to waste time speaking to people who have no interest or need for your services. So, make sure you check if there's a fit first. Networking at conferences is a numbers game. You'll have to meet a ton of people to make good connections. So be patient and be prepared to introduce yourself a lot. Remember to smile since it can get tough to wade through all of the potentially non-lucrative contacts you'll make.

How do you find conferences taking place? The easiest way is to head over to Google and type "trucking conferences", "trucking events", or some variation of those phrases. You can also inquire on forums or Facebook groups. Your LinkedIn feed will also contain posts from people advertising the conferences their companies are sponsoring or where they'll be speaking. So, make sure you connect with as many people as possible there!

You can also check websites such as fleetowner.com, eventsamerica.com, ttnews.com, and 10times.com. There are other industry publications that will have their own events. You can find them by searching for "transportation publications", "logistics publications", "trucking publications", and so on.

Freight Brokers and Dispatchers

Most truckers end up using intermediaries to find work since they don't have the time to carry out traditional marketing. An intermediary is a great resource you can use but you'll be reducing your overall earnings by using them. It's the cost of doing business. Freight brokers are intermediaries and will give you a steady stream of work. The key is to pick the right ones. There are many freight brokers out there who are incompetent and will waste your time. A good freight broker will work with quality truckers so it's essential that you present yourself as one. Check with other truckers and get recommendations for good brokers to work with. The key to working well with a broker is to first check whether they're legitimate and second, to evaluate their regulatory knowledge. Many freight brokers operate a boiler-room-style operation where securing loads is the key. These places don't care much about the trucker or the issues they need to contend with. As a result, if you haul for these places, you'll have to deal with all the regulatory headaches. This is especially a problem if you're hauling HAZMAT. Check to see if their MC number is valid and operational. A good freight broker will interview you as if you're applying to be their employee. This is a good thing since it shows they're thorough in their work. Ask them questions about how long they've been in business and how well they understand their work. Ask them regulatory questions if it applies to your niche. Ask for references of other truckers they work with and contact those people to get feedback. A good freight broker will also ensure you get paid in a reasonable time period. Typically, this is 60 days. A bad broker will pay you after 90 days, if they ever manage to get around to it. The freight brokering business is a small one, so you'll likely begin to hear about these people at some point. The best way to deal with your broker is to communicate clearly and always let them know that you'll abide by regulations. A broker who wants you to relax your HOS requirements or any other legality should not be trusted. After all, you're the one who'll pay the penalty. Don't be afraid to haggle rates with them. Freight brokers usually earn a margin of 18% on their loads. This means the difference in the price they receive from the shipper and the price they quote you is 18%. Shipper rates aren't always known but you can research them by talking to shippers and networking with them. Negotiate down to the 18% difference with freight brokers. They might create a fuss, but they'll usually agree to this. Another intermediary that helps truckers find loads is a truck dispatcher. You can hire a dispatcher yourself and task them with finding you loads, or you can hire a firm. Many dispatch firms provide back-office services such as bookkeeping and invoice collection. If you're looking for an all in one solution that can save you time figuring out how to organize your back office, you should look into working with these firms. However, like with freight brokers, this relationship has a price. A dispatcher will work with 18% margins just like freight brokers do. Conduct your research into the dispatcher's operations by asking for references and talking to other truckers. This will help you avoid bad dispatchers. The final option for securing loads is to sign up as a government contractor. This is an opportunity that is increasing as time goes by. There is a shortage of qualified truckers and local governments are looking for reliable trucking service providers. Signing up as a government contractor involves a few additional steps but it's worth it. The process varies from one county to another so check with your local government authorities.

Conclusion

There are many benefits to starting a trucking business. The biggest advantage is that there is a definite shortage of qualified truckers who can haul loads. The other advantage is that the profit margins in the trucking business are well known.

The average trucking business earns 30.30 cents per mile in the United States and costs average out to 25 cents per mile (Rodela, 2018). This means you stand to earn a clear profit of five cents per mile.

A key requirement to succeed in this business is the willingness to work hard and to plan your marketing strategy much before you hit the road.

Many truck owners stick to tired old marketing tactics and fail to adopt new methods. Right now, you have a huge opportunity if you can successfully execute an online marketing strategy.

This will help you skip past the intermediaries and directly get in touch with shippers. You'll earn more and will even be able to transition to a career of brokering your own freight should you tire of driving a truck.

So, what are the costs involved? Here's a detailed breakdown:

Item	Cost
Business setup	$500
Licenses and authority	$500
CDL and tags	$3,000 (maximum)
Office setup (includes furniture, computer, and other equipment)	$1,500
Other permits (IFTA, Heavy use vehicle taxes etc)	$2,000 (maximum)
Equipment cost	$10,000 down payment on truck
Compliance devices cost (ELD)	$1,000
Total costs	$18,500

The costs listed in the table above assume you're running a one-person owner-operator shop. If you hire employees and run multiple vehicles, these costs will increase. A lot also depends on how you choose to finance your truck.

You can reduce your costs by borrowing more money to lease your truck or you can front-load your costs and buy your truck with cash. While startup costs are reasonable, the running costs of a trucking business are harder to estimate. A common rule of thumb is to assume you'll spend $1.50 per mile driven. This includes maintenance costs as well as any other emergency expenses that you might encounter. Your office costs can be decreased as I mentioned previously by splitting it with other owner-operators. You could even hire a single person to manage all of the back-office tasks you might need fulfilling.

I haven't included the cost of TMS software in the office costs in the table above. Marketing costs are also not included since so much depends on how you choose to go about executing your strategy. The most effective method is to rely on LinkedIn and run email newsletters. This doesn't cost you anything other than paying a monthly fee of around $20 for a website platform. Attending conferences and trade shows might cost you money but you can mitigate this by attending online events that are free of charge. Networking on forums and Facebook groups is also free so marketing charges don't add up to much, unless you spend a lot of money on paid social media ads.

Before you begin your business, take some time to figure out your marketing plan and how you'll schedule your activities. The best way to do this is to assign a single task every day of the week. For example, you could work on LinkedIn networking on Mondays, conduct your interview strategy on Tuesday, network on groups and forums on Wednesday, record a video on Thursday, edit it on Friday, and upload it on Saturday.

All you need to do is spend 30 minutes every day on your marketing. This doesn't sound like a lot of time, but you need to account for driving as well. Obviously, you shouldn't be carrying out your marketing tasks when driving or doing anything else for that matter other than driving at those times. However, thanks to the prevalence of mobile data packages and the internet, you can successfully execute these tasks on the road. Attend conferences once a month, either physically or online. Many forums have physical meetups so make sure you attend those as well. Keep executing your marketing bit by bit every day, and you'll reap the rewards.

The trucking business is a tough one for sure. However, with the strategies I've given you in this book, you'll manage to sidestep many of the mistakes that beginners make. Many truckers are still stuck in the past when it comes to running their business' day-to-day operations. You need to be creative and work hard to succeed these days. The strategies in this book will help you do just that.

It isn't enough for you to just read everything that has been presented here. It's now time for you to get out there and start taking action. You will meet with hurdles along the way so make sure you keep coming back to this book and refer to what you need to do. The most important thing to remember is that no matter how large the hurdles are, other successful owner-operators have overcome them. This means you can do so as well. I'm positive you've learned a ton of valuable information in this book. Let me know what you think by leaving me a review. I wish you all the luck in the world and hope to hear about your successful trucking venture soon!

References

Hours of Service. (2013, December 30). Federal Motor Carrier Safety Administration. https://www.fmcsa.dot.gov/regulations/hours-of-service

How do I get a Commercial Driver's License? | FMCSA. (2020). Www.Fmcsa.Dot.Gov. https://www.fmcsa.dot.gov/registration/commercial-drivers-license/how-do-i-get-commercial-drivers-license

License and Permit Checklist for Starting a Trucking Company. (2020). Www.Rtsinc.com. https://www.rtsinc.com/guides/license-and-permit-checklist-starting-trucking-company

Rodela, J. (2018, October 23). *How much does it cost to start your trucking business?* KeepTruckin. https://keeptruckin.com/blog/cost-starting-trucking-business

Step by Step Guide to Getting Your Trucking Insurance. (2020). Process Agent. https://www.processagent.com/insurance

Warnes, B. (2020). *What is a Sole Proprietorship? (A Complete Guide) | Bench Accounting.* Bench. https://bench.co/blog/operations/sole-proprietorship

Wescott, S. (2019, June 24). *Understanding Commercial Truck Insurance.* Merchant Maverick.

https://www.merchantmaverick.com/understanding-commercial-truck-insurance/

Zaryzcki, N. (2020). *C Corporations: Everything You Need to Know | Bench Accounting.* Bench. https://bench.co/blog/operations/c-corporation

All images from Pixabay